AN
ILLUSTRATION
OF GRACE

AN ILLUSTRATION OF GRACE

KARLA FIAONI

GABRIELPRESS

An Illustration of Grace
Copyright © 2011 by Karla Fiaoni

International Standard Book Number: 978-0-9835597-0-2
Library of Congress Catalog Number: 2011940985

Front cover photo by author

Back cover photo shot by Doyle Designed
and Jennifer Orr Photography

PRINTED IN THE UNITED STATES OF AMERICA

GABRIEL PRESS

This book is dedicated to my mom.

FOREWORD

I am not certain where my grandmother first heard it or even her grandmother before that, but most of us have heard it told, in one variation or another, to "give a person their roses before they die." I consider this book to be a spiritual bouquet of roses for us, the reader.

When our lives present challenges and obstacles, how easy it would be to walk down that path that would leave us feeling isolated, alone and not feeling worthy of love—love from one another, love from God. Karla's story helps us realize that this love, which may seemingly appear absent from our lives, is there in abundance. This courageously told story helps us come face to face with the demons present in our world, in our local communities, in our families, even in ourselves. Yet through it all, God's love continues to weave throughout our lives, oftentimes using the voices of others to help us come to grips with this reality.

Whether you are or have been the victim of violence or abuse of any type, or know of someone who is, know that you are never alone. God sends people into our lives to draw us to Him, to let us know that we are worthy of His love. Karla tells a story of how God is with us, not in some superficial, abstract way, but in ways that are very real and intimate. This book demonstrates how and from whom we can draw our strength—from family, friends, neighbors, co-workers, and our churches and places of worship.

To know that we are never alone is perhaps one of the greatest gifts many of us can receive from God. One of the most beautiful ways to understand this is how many of us pray. For many the posture of our prayer is with our hands folded, still for others it is with our hands out, and our palms open. This second form is a posture of receiving—our hands are open and ready to receive the gifts of God. Oftentimes, these hands are filled with the hands of another. Our hands joined together, in prayer, to receive love and also to share it. Not only do we receive the gifts of God and God's blessings, but we are compelled to become a source of God's presence and blessings for another whose hands are also reaching up.

Receive this book into your lives as you would receive a rose from a friend. Cherish it. Take comfort in it. Draw strength from it. Absorb the sweet fragrance of God's love, of God's presence and of God's grace.

Father Kevin Birmingham

GRACE OF GOD

There but for the grace of God, go I. I wonder how many of us know how true it really is. The hope of this book is to send encouragement to victims of abuse and hope to all God's children, so they may accept God's grace which is there for us all.

Abuse committed against children by a pedophile relative or a stranger does not happen in a vacuum. If it did happen to you or someone you love, it did not happen to you alone. What does this mean?

I have come to learn that Jesus is with us always.

He says, "I am with you always" and He means just that.

So if this is true, and I believe that it is, then He was with me since the day I was born, no, with me even in my mother's womb, and hence, He was with me the night my father abused me. He is with me now and with you as you read this book.

Although it may not have seemed like it at the time, the truth is that Jesus was right there in the room with me, while the abuse was going on that night. That is the only way I could have survived it. How else could any eight-year-old child survive what my father did to me but for Jesus and all his angels standing with me and helping me to survive it.

• • •

For years, I would not, could not, take myself back to that night because I had always thought it was just me and my pedophile father in that bedroom. Once I realized that Jesus was with me crying with me, and helping me to get out of that room as soon as I could...either by sending an angel to make a noise or tipping over a pot that would make my father think that someone was coming...I understood that *He*, Jesus, got me out of there as quickly as possible and that He had the love I needed to heal. Our Lord is merciful. But because Jesus does not get in front of our free will, He did not get in front of my father's free will either. But in His mercy, some forty-five years later, I look back at that night and understand that, He, Jesus, stayed with me all night. He, Jesus, gave me the courage in the morning to tell my mother what my father had done to me. He, Jesus, gave my mother the clarity to understand that I was telling the truth. And Jesus finally gave my mother the strength to throw my dad out.

I wish I could say that we then lived happily ever after, but some of the darkest days were yet to come. The devil himself was not satisfied with the attempted destruction of a family and an eight-year-old child. That was not good enough; he wanted the destruction of our entire family. And in my father he had a willing partner.

Of course I would like to believe that my dad, Stan, was not always a willing partner to the devil and there actually was another helper known as Seagram's 7, Stan's drink of choice. I would like to think that Stan would not have followed the devil so willingly down this path if he had not always had his little friend Seagram's 7 with him. I would like to think that being in a drunken stupor most of the time blurred things for him and that if he had been sober he may have been able to resist the devil's evil suggestions. I would also like to think that Stan repented for his sins prior to his death.

SUMMER OF '56

I was born at a hospital where the nurses refused to assist my mother in my birth because the doctor had not arrived. They said they were not allowed to start the "delivery process" without the doctor present. Really? Well, no one told me about those hospital rules, so when it was time for me to be born, I came so quickly that no one was there to assist. My mother, Julie, says, "Karla knew it was her time."

I was the second of four children. I had one brother, Keith, who was eleven months older than I. I was followed by two younger sisters, Darla, who came two years later, and finally Donna who arrived four years after that.

We all lived in a house owned by my paternal grandparents on the Near North side of Chicago in an area now known as Ukrainian Village. The home was actually a two-story bungalow which had two separate apartments. My family lived in the upstairs three-bedroom apartment, and my dad's parents and sister lived in the basement two-bedroom apartment below.

My mom, Julie, had her hands full as a stay at home mom raising four children who were so close in age.

My dad, Stanley, was a less than perfect husband and father. He was a drinker, a gambler, a womanizer, and involved with the Mafia. He ran a bookie operation from our dining room table, taking illegal bets on sporting events.

My mom tried very hard to shield us from my dad's bad habits and illegal operations, but the frequent visits by local law enforcement made that a challenge. But since we thought everyone lived that way, it really didn't bother us kids that much.

I remember one night playing the board game Yahtzee at the dining room table with my grandmother and siblings when right in the middle of the game, the police kicked in our front door and collected all the paperwork they could find for evidence in their case incriminating my dad's bookie operation. They even took our Yahtzee score sheets as evidence of a gambling operation. Little did they know that the little girl sitting at the table, whose Yahtzee sheets they had just confiscated, was the future chief of police of Chicago Heights.

THE MEN IN MY WORLD

My dad worked in the Movie Projectionist Union just like his father, who was a Polish immigrant. He changed his name from Dakowski to Dutton. He said it was an attempt to assimilate into the movie projectionist union which was dominated by the Italians. He had changed his name, we were told, because he wanted to sound less like an immigrant and more like an American. I think it was because he enjoyed having two different names which he turned into two different identities, which served him well in his illegal activities.

My brother, Keith, eventually followed my dad into his line of work and ended up working in the movie Projectionist union as well. He eventually served jail time for his "work" in the union. My father escaped the FBI and jail time when he died an untimely death in 1989. They came looking for him weeks later, and my aunt simply said he was "not home." She was so accustomed to lying to the police for him that it came naturally even after we buried him. I remember thinking, just tell them he is dead, but it never occurred to my aunt, who had spent her life covering up for her little brother.

A LINE OF STRONG WOMEN

I come from a line of very strong women. My grandmothers were very different women and came from very different worlds. I like to think that I inherited the best qualities of each of them.

MOM'S MOM

Grandma Bernice was a Fitzgerald, Irish as the day is long and tough as nails, or at least that's how she appeared to me as a child.

She had to be tough because when she was just sixteen she married Judd Chilton, a much older French and English man, who gave her the "opportunity" to have ten children in just fourteen years and then revealed his own very abusive ways with the girls. My Grandma Bernice threw him out, with a butcher knife in hand, when it was finally revealed that he had been going into the girls' room at night. She never looked back.

Unfortunately, Grandma Bernice could not raise all ten of the kids on a waitress' salary, and the children ended up separated: some in orphanages and some in foster homes. My mom, Julie (Fitzgerald) Chilton, was just a young girl when the family split up. As always, God was looking out for our family. Julie was taken into the foster care of a young couple, who just happened to be the minister and his wife at Erie House, just down the street from where they lived. Not long after she moved in with them, they moved to the State of Washington, and Julie finished out her teenage years in relative calm while in the care of this wonderful couple and their young children. Julie was raised in the Church, the Swedish Covenant Church. (Later in life my mom's foster mother has a granddaughter who is down on her luck, and my sister Darla has offered her a place to live; God's circle of grace continues.)

MY DAD'S MOTHER— MAE SCHAFER-DATKOWSKI

Grandma Dutton was actually Mae Schafer from Germany. She married Stanley Datkowski. They were married for many, many years until the day he died. They had three children. My dad was the only boy and the baby. Possibly that added to his spoiled nature and lack of self-control. I heard many stories of how my grandmother would never ever let my grandfather discipline him. One time my grandfather grabbed a belt and was going to tan Stan's hide. My grandmother actually got in front of her son and took the lashing herself. I do not know if this is true, but that was the family legend. I do not advocate belt beatings for children or anyone, but I guess this pattern of behavior may help explain why my father behaved the way he did.

Another family story that bears repeating is when my father was fifteen years old and he was out joy riding with his father's car. He struck a young immigrant boy playing in the street. The accident killed the immigrant boy. My grandparents quickly paid off the boy's family and then sent my father away to the merchant marines at only fifteen years old with a false birth certificate.

Grandpa Dutton died when I was just a baby, and Grandma Dutton spent the rest of her years taking care of everybody, but especially my father. She worked at the local Wiebolt's Department Store and still managed to clean and cook for her grown children. I loved her so much, and I was sure she loved me right back. She spent her life telling me that I was special and smart and wonderful and destined to do great things. At times, I even believed her. All was right with the world when I was with my grandma.

A "NORMAL" CHILDHOOD

My first memories of childhood are normal childhood days with my brother and sisters, playing and having fun. I loved school and excelled so much that I skipped the third grade at seven years old and went from second to fourth grade. This was the trend in those days, to double-promote the smart kids.

We lived in a neighborhood where no one had central air. In the summertime, most of the parents and grandparents sat out on the front porch and visited while the kids played up and down the block running around pretty much free as the birds. Fast forward to 2011 and my grandson. Never could I think of him with such freedom. Although I see now how much we lacked worldly goods, at the time it did not matter to us. All that mattered was that we had a safe place to go to sleep at night and enough food to eat and parents who loved us. This is also true today, yet we seem to struggle to provide *more things* for our kids, when what they really need is *more of us*. What wisdom comes from being a grandparent. Wow.

THE FATHER MOMENT

One of my childhood memories occurred when I was four years old. It was a December night, and my parents had sent all of us kids to bed. My dad was in the living room watching TV, and my mom was in the kitchen washing clothes. We had a roller washer that she had to hook up to the sink.

My brother and I shared a bedroom, and when we were sent to bed that night, we were anything but tired. We were having a ball goofing around. We jumped on the beds, back and forth. All of the blankets and sheets had fallen to the floor. In all of this horseplay, I managed to rip off one of the buttons of the mattress. Yikes! What should I do now?! After a few more "Quiet down in there" hollers from my dad, which we ignored, I could hear his footsteps coming down the hall. I knew we would get in big trouble if he saw the button off of the mattress. I didn't have any pockets in my pajamas, so I did what any four-year-old would do in this state of fear—I shoved it up my nose. I feared him because he was scary and loud and always seemed a bit unstable even to a four-year-old. Literally, I shoved it up my nose, so it must have been a small button. My brother decided that a button up the nose was serious business, so he told my mom and dad. My mom took a look and did what little she could and then decided it was time to call the doctor.

Now in the 1960s, it was customary for a family to have one doctor who took care of everything and everybody in the family. Dr. Yaney had been taking care of our family for generations. When his phone rang, late in the evening, and he found out that little Karla had stuck a button up her nose, he told my parents to bring me straight to his office, and he would meet us there. Yes, at night, we were going to his office. He agreed to meet us there in good old Oak Park, Illinois, a nice suburb of Chicago, about twenty minutes away by car. My mom called my Grandma Dutton to come to watch the other kids. Now it was just me, my mom, and my dad, and we headed off to Dr. Yaney's office.

Dr. Yaney took one look up my nose and said, "It has to come out. We're just going to put a wire up her nose and yank it out." I started to scream. My mom was looking at me with concern, and my dad was holding me in his arms and saying over and over, "It is okay, Karla, it is okay. It is okay." He was trying to soothe me and talk me down. I was screaming bloody murder as Dr. Yaney was working diligently up my nose. Well, this went on for quite a while. Dr. Yaney never did get that button out of my nose. (About six months later I had a horrible cold, and all it took was a one serious sneeze and out it flew.)

Driving home that night I felt like I was loved. I thought I am one lucky little girl. I thought that maybe that scary, loud, unstable dad was gone and a nice one had appeared in his place. I was wrong. It was just a moment when good had triumphed over evil, but evil was to return, and quickly.

Fifty years later, that is the only memory of my dad ever behaving like a real father should. And that is what I held on to for an image of a good dad, a good and caring, loving father. It makes me smile now when I think of that evening because I have a good sense of what God the Father is and has always been in my life. God holding me in His arms, saying over and over again, "It is okay, Karla, it is okay." Calling me by name, telling me it's okay, soothing me, talking me down when I am screaming bloody murder as life is diligently up my nose. I just realized that, again—wow, isn't God great?!

Yes, it would be nice to have had an earthly father just like the one that God meant for me to have. Oh yes, just like the one He meant for you to have as well, and some people do in fact have that dad here on earth. *Some do not.* But we all have God our Father in Heaven. And when we finally realize this truth, it is so very calming and peaceful to the soul.

• • •

I do not pretend to get it right 100 percent of the time, or even close. I do keep constant reminders all around my home so that I do not have a moment where I can forget that God is with me always, even unto the end of time. I find it comforting to have rosaries all around the house. Pictures of our Jesus and our beloved Blessed Mother Mary and some of the saints remind me day in and day out of the fact that God our Father loves us so much that He sent His only Son to die for us and to rise again after three days in that tomb.

I heard a song the other day about Jesus spending nine months in his mother's womb and then three days in a borrowed tomb. Singer Francesca Battistelli thanks him for the "time in between." Absolutely spot on, I must say. So what am I doing with the "time in between"? Well, trying to write this book for one, and trying everyday to let Jesus shine through my soul and worship and honor my Father in heaven. Failing miserably on some days. Falling down and getting back up. Falling down, getting back up, dusting off my knees, and trying again. I am not ashamed to fall down, and I am not afraid to get up. Why? Because Jesus has my back. Actually, He has my elbow most days, helping me back up. Maybe that is why God made elbows, so that here on earth the people who try to help us back up as will have something to hold on to.

THAT NIGHT

Things seemed pretty normal to me until one summer night when I was eight. My normal was about to change. My mother had decided to go to a wedding reception of a friend or relative, I am not sure which, but what I am sure of is that the children were left at home and my father was to stay home with us that evening. We went to bed that evening, and it seemed uneventful. Then at some point I was awakened by my father. I was taken from my bed and carried into his bedroom. Scared and confused at his requests, I just wanted to go back to sleep in my own bed.

This was not to be, however, and his requests soon turned to commands and orders which I tried to refuse. I started to cry. The next thing I remember is being slapped in the face. This, of course, did not stop my crying. Why do abusers think that more abuse will stop the crying? With a bloody nose and tear-stained face I was returned to my bed with a stern warning that I must not tell my mother or anyone about what he did to me that night.

My assigned angels must have soothed me to sleep that night, while I hugged my pillow. When I woke up the next morning, I stayed in my bed and pretended to remain asleep. I waited until I heard my father get up and leave the house. My mom came into my room to see why I was still in bed. I told her what had occurred that night. She saw the crusted blood and tear stains on my face and pillow. *She knew.* She knew I was telling the truth, and she knew what he had done. It broke her heart. Not because she loved him so much or anything like that. She had learned over the past nine years just what a bum he was. It broke her heart because she knew how I felt. She knew exactly how I felt. She knew I would never be "a little girl" again. She knew life for all of us was about to change forever.

JULIE GETS ANGRY

My mom was devastated, and she was also very angry. She was kind of like the Incredible Hulk. She was always the nicest sweetest lady in the world, but, like the Hulk, you really did not want to make her angry, and angry she was.

My mom packed us kids up, and we headed for Oak Street Beach. The Oak Street Beach was just one bus ride away, straight down Chicago Avenue. Thinking back, it was an excellent idea. My siblings could play in the sand and in the water. In 1964 the water and the beach seemed pristine, and my mom and I could talk about what lay ahead.

No doubt about it, I was all grown up overnight. You cannot survive if you look back. She called my dad from a pay phone. In 1964 there were no cell phones. I overheard her say, "*Stan, I know what you did to Karla. You better move out today. If you are there when I get back tonight, I will kill you myself.*" Wow. Now that is a strong woman. I felt safe at that moment, protected. Julie had learned this kind of strength from my Grandma Bernice.

And so my dad did move out that day. But alas, he did not go far. He moved downstairs into the apartment with his mother and his sister. No kidding. That really sucked. And it was about to get even worse.

My mom told his mother, my Grandma Dutton, and his sister, my Aunt Estelle, what he had done to me and why she threw him out. To her surprise, they did not believe her. They did not want to believe her. Looking back, who *would* want to believe that their son or brother could be capable of such evil? It was much easier to simply accuse me of being a hysterical child and a liar. My dad has always denied that night ever happened, even to the day he died.

YOU DO THE MATH

The three of them, Grandma Dutton, Auntie Estelle, and my dad soon decided they were just too crowded in the rat-infested basement apartment below us. So they decided that my mom, I, and my three siblings should move down there instead and let them live upstairs in the three-bedroom bigger apartment.

My mom had no job, little training except a high school typing class, no money, and no prospect for a job. We moved into the basement apartment while she looked for a job and relied on my Grandma Dutton to give us money for groceries. My father refused to consider the idea that my mom was never coming back to him and instead thought he could just "starve" us into returning.

He underestimated my mom and her Irish determination, as well as her Christian upbringing. We were never going back, and she would never subject her children to his abuse again. My mom found work in the neighborhood. She had no welfare and received no food stamps. She just worked. I tried to help her the best that I could at eight years old. After all, we were in this mess because of what my father had done to me. I thought it only right for me to help her as best I could. Anyway, I was almost nine years old by then.

Living in the basement while my abusive father lived upstairs proved to be an absolute disaster. I would wake up in the middle of the night, screaming from nightmares. My father came downstairs several times a week, trying to twist my mother's arm to get her to return. No joke, he would literally grab her arm and twist it behind her back and try to make her agree to return. How stupid is that? But it is the truth.

THE DREAM KEEPER

My mom knew things were getting worse for me, and she knew I needed help. But what could she do? She could barely put food on the table. My father continued to believe that we would all be back when the going got too tough. My mother never backed down, and we never went back. The nightmares continued, and no matter what we tried, I would wake up every night screaming. Of course, it did not help that my abuser lived upstairs. I needed professional help, and my mother knew it. A child psychologist was needed, and that would not be cheap. Somehow my mother scraped together one hundred dollars and found a female psychologist who agreed to provide four sessions for twenty-five bucks apiece. It had to work. It had to be enough. That was all she had. My mom explained everything to the child psychologist and that she really needed this to work. Period. My mom was not college educated or polished and was not in the mood to be turned away.

The psychologist was very kind to me. She taught me some very important coping skills and introduced me to the concept of the "Dream Keeper." She explained to me that throughout the day I might think about bad things and sad things. When this happened and I did not want to think about them, I simply pushed them aside and out of my mind and tried to focus on better and happier things. Well, she explained, when you push these things aside, they go into a place known as the Dream Keeper. All these upsetting thoughts stay there all day. But, when you lie down to sleep and you begin to dream, all of those bad, scary and sad thoughts come out of the Dream Keeper and that is why you have bad dreams and nightmares. She told me I needed to empty the Dream Keeper out while I was still awake. Then there would be nothing left, no bad thoughts to fill my dreams with. She said it was really easy to do. I should practice it every day, and soon the bad dreams would go away. That's pretty good for only four sessions and one hundred bucks.

So in order to stop dreaming about all these bad things, on *that* night, I would have to stop and think about them during the day. Yes, whenever I would start to remember what happened that night, I would stop and actually really think about what happened that night, see the images, hear his words, Yikes, relive it while I was awake. I could only do this for about sixty seconds at a time, and then I would get sick to my stomach. But, hey, it worked. I emptied the Dream Keeper of all the thoughts and fears of that night every day in class. I treated it like homework. No matter what was going on in class, I took time to relive it and empty the Dream Keeper. And, after a while, it worked. It really worked. No more nightmares. The only downside was that I missed a lot of class time while I zoned-out, and no one knew why.

BEST FRIENDS
(BUT NOT FOREVER)

lthough we originally went to public school, my mom transferred us to St. John's Lutheran just around the corner and down one block from where we lived. We attended Church there every Sunday, and my mom tried to participate as much as she could in the Parent Teacher League (PTL) while working and raising four kids. She knew we would not survive in a secular environment.

My best friend in fifth grade was Susana, who lived a few blocks away. Her mom and dad were also very active in the school and church. One night after a potluck dinner, Susana and I found our way to a private area in the school. We needed privacy because we needed to talk. I figured that if my Dream Keeper could be controlled with simple daytime thoughts, then it might be possible to eliminate it all together if I could just actually talk about what happened and say it out loud without bursting into tears. I thought, who better to try this with but my best friend? So off we went to find a secret place in the school where no would find us and no one else would ever even know we were there. We ended up under some stairs in the lower level. There was just enough room for two little fifth graders under the stairs, and we agreed that this was the most super-secret conversation ever. In fact, I had never told a soul. So there we were, sworn to secrecy, and I thought, here goes. As I was telling her, she remained calm. We discussed how brave I was to tell my mom. The bigger question, which had been on my mind forever, was, could I get pregnant from what he made me do? And if not, then what the heck do you have to do to get pregnant because this was gross enough.

Neither of us could even imagine anything worse that what had occurred to me. Susana did not have an answer to the pregnancy question so we decided to pull in a seventh grader who might know the answer. Of course, we couldn't tell her *why* we wanted to know. We would somehow get her to tell us just how babies were made. She had to know. She was in seventh grade for goodness' sake. So we sought her out and invited her to our secret place under the stairs and began the conversation. After her lengthy description of what she knew, I was finally at ease. I learned two things. One, there was no way I could have gotten pregnant from what happened that night. And, two, there was no way I was *ever* going to do the things she described. Both Susana and I swore we would never ever do that yucky gross stuff.

STAN CONTINUES HIS REIGN OF TERROR

My mom, my sisters and brother and I were living in the basement apartment which was very crowded and very dangerous. My dad kept coming downstairs and trying to get us to open the door when my mom was at work. Even our large German shepherd/collie mix dog, Frisky, was afraid of him. My mom's brother, Uncle Truman, was just back from the Navy. He tried to stay with us as much as he could. Unfortunately, he was no match for a drunken, self-righteous, stupid idiot, aka my dad, who thought he was the injured party in all this.

And just when you may think it was safe to go back in the water, my dad convinced my sainted Grandma Dutton that if she would just serve my mom with an eviction notice, yes, an eviction notice, then my mom would have no choice but to return to him and his financial support. Honest. I kid you not. Yes, the devil can work wonders with Seagram's 7 and Stupid.

But God had already put His plan into motion, and when my mom got the eviction notice, she simply found an apartment a few blocks away on Cortez Street. The best part of this was that my best friend, Susana, lived right across the street. The worse part of this was that the new place was really small. It was a two-bedroom, four-room apartment. With four kids it was extremely tight. And we were very noisy kids. This arrangement did not last long. My mom spoke with two elderly women from the church we attended and they offered her a larger apartment. Not just any apartment, an apartment she could actually afford on her meager salary from the desk job at the YMCA. This apartment had three bedrooms, it was back on our old block, and it was right across the street from my abuser. So we moved.

BACK ON RICE STREET

I was ten years old. I was living right across the street from my abuser. But, hey, I was still in the same school, and my mom was the best. My mom asked me for my help with the younger kids and the laundry and the grocery shopping and the cleaning. I automatically agreed to do whatever I could to help her. From my perspective as a ten-year-old, she had saved my life. In many ways I felt like it was my fault we were in this predicament.

My brother Keith and my sisters had no idea why we moved out or why my mom was getting a divorce. At some point I think my brother figured out that it had something to do with me because I would run the other way if we saw my dad on the street in the neighborhood.

But all the craziness took a toll on my mom and my family. My brother Keith soon figured out that Stan was a nut. Like every little boy, he also feared that he was destined to be just like his dad. My mom was determined that her son have some hope. She eventually told him the hidden truth. Stan was *not* his biological father. Keith's real dad was an Italian man. Keith was thrilled to discover that he did not carry the crazy gene but extremely disappointed to discover that this guy did not accept the fact that he was his father. My brother never got over that rejection he felt from him.

My brother Keith may not have gotten the crazy gene by blood, but he ended up spending so much time with Stan, the only dad he ever knew, that he started to accept Stan's behavior as normal. It was a bad idea to defend Stan's behavior and accept it as normal. My brother and I grew apart.

While my father was busy trying to get my mom to reunite with him, she was busy trying to survive. The divorce went through, and we all just accepted life as it was day by day. School was a safe place. We learned about God's love for us and the sacrifice of His Son. Our school had beautiful pictures of Jesus everywhere. You know Him, the beautiful blond blue-eyed Jesus, the German version of Jesus for the Lutheran Church. Since I was blond and blue-eyed, it made sense to me at the time. I never considered that Jerusalem might have given us a darker skinned Jesus. I loved Him and He loved me, and that was all that mattered.

My best friend Susana had moved away. Her father wanted to move his family out of Chicago to the suburbs where his children would have a better life. That's what a father does. I was happy for her but sad for me. I had other friends at St. John's so I would just make a new best friend. After all, a girl has to have a best friend.

RICH OR POOR, WHO KNEW?

By 1969 most of the kids at St. John's were taking the bus to school because they lived too far from school to walk. We were one of the few neighborhood families that still attended St. John's. A lot of people were moving out of the neighborhood, and it was going downhill fast. But at twelve years old, I didn't understand that aspect of it. All I really knew was that a lot of the kids were coming from the projects (public low income housing), and they were black.

My new best friend in eighth grade was Valerie. She lived in the projects, and I never went to her house. Her mom worked just like my mom, and friends were not allowed in her house when her mom was not home. Valerie was smart and tall and skinny and just beautiful. She wanted to be a model someday. She knew what she wanted to be when she grew up. Me, not so much. I figured that I might just be a child psychologist. I could help kids, and I could have my own office and it would have a refrigerator with Coca Cola in it. I had no idea how it would happen, but I figured that it was a good thing to be and that God would work it out for me. So I did not spend any time on career planning.

We were busy at home just trying to pay the bills. I say *we* were too busy because I had become my mother's helper in every way. I was twelve, for goodness' sake, that's practically all grown up. I did some of the shopping and the laundry. My mom was counting on me to help make things work. We did the grocery list together and planned out the budget.

One day my mom and I went shopping on Chicago Avenue to buy a new coat for me for eighth grade. I had never had a new coat for school. My mom's foster mother, Mrs. Cedarleaf, had a daughter six years older than me, and she always gave us all of her clothing. Who needed something new? But this was eighth grade; my mom knew I needed a new coat. Somehow we would afford it. I picked out a brown cape coat. Not very practical, but really really cool. The coat was chocolate brown, really beautiful. It was a wraparound coat with big brown buttons and a big cool collar. I could not wait to wear it to school and hang it up in the coat room for all to see. I was sure I looked like a model.

I never realized that we were poor. I didn't realize that I never had new clothes until I wore the new brown coat to school. When the bell rang at the end of the school day, I went to get my coat. All I could hear was gossip talk from some of the other girls: That couldn't be Karla's new coat. It's brand new and really cool. Whose coat was it *really* because Karla *never* has new stuff? Well, it was mine. I was no longer happy about it. I was pissed off. How dare they accuse me of taking someone else's coat. Well, they could call my mom and ask her if they didn't believe me. Valerie believed me, but even she was shocked that my mom had been able to afford the new coat.

Everyone knew we were poor but us. That was the day I found out.

DIVORCING A CONNECTED GUY

Divorcing a connected guy is not as easy as you would think. My dad was connected all right, connected to the guys in the movie projection union. My grandfather had been a union movie projectionist, and my father was accepted into the union on that basis. My brother as well became a union movie projectionist, and membership had its advantages. They were a very closed club, they got paid very well, and they very well-connected.

My dad always wanted to get back together with my mom even after the divorce. Of course, my mom wanted nothing to do with him and tried to live her life as best she could. She even went out on a date with Vince, the brother of one of her childhood friends. That relationship ended when Vince's car was firebombed the night after he had been out with her. No one wanted to mess around with my dad and his friends. But that did not end my dad's ruthless pursuit of my mom. The next weekend he showed up at our door with a hatchet. He said that if she would not let him in, he would chop the door down. No joke. Truth is stranger than fiction, and you cannot make this stuff up. That incident, along with the firebombing of Vince's car who never called her again, was enough for my mom to decide to move us away, far away from Rice Street and crazytown USA across the street.

A PRO-CHOICE FEMI-NAZI AT THIRTEEN YEARS OLD

While I was still in eighth grade going to graduate soon, my mom confided in me that a very close friend of hers was very sick because she had been pregnant. Because of her circumstances, divorced from another neighborhood crazy, this woman decided to get an abortion, a back alley abortion as they were called in 1969. I knew this woman very well. I babysat for her children. I had spent many nights at her house. She was very kind to me, and I loved her dearly. In fact, I was called over to babysit at her house while she was in the hospital, after almost bleeding to death after the abortion. I helped out by watching her kids for a few days after she came home. I was very sad for my mom's friend and very angry that someone would perform a back alley abortion on a woman and let her almost bleed to death. What kind of a world is this? I thought. This sucks (my favorite phrase).

My mom's friend recovered, and news spread pretty fast in the neighborhood. This was wrong, I thought, not really sure why. This experience led to my overzealous pro-choice attitude in my twenties and thirties. I had turned into a femi-Nazi.

I thank God for His grace. I am sure He just tolerated my attitude as you tolerate that of a teenager because He had the wisdom that "this too shall pass."

HIGH SCHOOL

n the fall of 1969, I began my freshman year at Luther North High School. I wanted to attend Luther North because my best friend Valerie was going there, not so much for the religious education. It was quite expensive, and my mom could not afford it. I made a decision to go and speak with my father and ask him to pay for it. After all, over five years had passed, and I was strong enough to go and face him and ask for the money. At least that is what I thought at the time, but I asked my mom to go with me. My father was delighted to meet with us and incorrectly took it as a sign that all was forgiven. NOT. We were careful not to say anything that would interfere with our getting the check for Luther North.

My freshman year was wild to say the least. I arrived at an almost all-white high school with my best friend, Valerie, who was African-American. Since I had gone to an integrated grade school and since both my parents had always had at least one black friend, I was in no way prepared for the segregation of the lunch room. The year 1969 was a very turbulent time in and of itself. The Viet Nam war was still going on. All the senior girls had gathered in the senior lounge to see if their boyfriends had been drafted. I had just gone through freshman orientation with my senior sister who was assigned to help me navigate my first year in high school. She never mentioned that there was a "black" lunch table in the cafeteria. When lunch time came, I looked for Valerie and sat down at the table with her to eat and talk. I did not know that it was the "black" table, but I was to find that out very soon after sitting down. The other black kids, whom I did not know, announced that this was the "black" table. I could hear some of the white kids commenting as well. To say I was stunned is an understatement. ***Black table?*** Are you kidding me? You have got to be kidding me!

No, they were not. Valerie and I were best friends. We were really close. So if I could not sit there, then she would not sit there. **Period**. So there. So I stayed there and ate my lunch and returned the next day and the next.

This did not make some of the white students very happy. I was told that if I continued to sit at the black table I would have to sit there all the time. **What?** What the heck kind of place is this? This is not right. Whatever! My friend was my friend. That was all there was to it. Valerie stuck up for me. I will not play this stupid game with these white kids. So there, I am at the black table forever. Period. This began my isolation from the white kids and my close ties to the black kids, who all eventually accepted me or so I was led to believe. Valerie and I stayed close, but she was very focused on academics and grades and that was just not my thing in high school. I could maintain a "C" average by just showing up, and I was constantly daydreaming in class in order to avoid the reality of what I would face when I got home.

My mom was working six days a week just to pay the rent and put food on the table. I was in charge of the rest. My uncles came over every now and then, and Grandma Bernice Fitzgerald would, too, but she was always pretty gruff and I just tried to stay out of her way.

My school clothes consisted of two green skirts, two green shirts, and a few pairs of socks and underwear. We were always washing out our underwear in the bathroom sink. We did not have enough to make it to the weekend trip to the laundromat.

STAN IS PERSISTENT, IF NOT TOO BRIGHT

It was during my freshman year that my dad got the foolish idea that because he had paid my high school tuition, it was time for him and my mom to reconcile. When she flatly refused, for the fifteenth time, he hired a high-priced lawyer and threatened to seek custody of my two younger sisters. That was the last straw for my mom. She would never let him get custody of my younger sisters. We devised a plan. It was decided that I would appear in court with her. I would tell the judge what he had done to me. Stan did not see that one coming. My mom told Stan's lawyer what he had done and that I was there with her because I was going to tell the judge myself what had occurred. His lawyer was flabbergasted. I remember him taking my dad outside in the hallway and screaming at him. My father withdrew his custody request and agreed to pay for the next three years at Luther North for me. (As it turned out, I dropped out in my junior year.) Stan knew we were not bluffing, and so did his lawyer. At thirteen years old, I was fully prepared to "spread of record" all the horrible details of that night. What the heck. It was true! As far as I was concerned, he would never get a chance at my little sisters.

Life went on. We moved up north. It was only two buses to Luther North each day instead of the three buses from Rice Street. My brother was going to Lakeview High School and was in the school band. It probably looked rather normal to most outsiders. What is really normal anyway?

We lived on Clark Street, just a block from Wrigley Field, the home of the Chicago Cubs. It was 1970, and the neighborhood had not gotten the attention or the wealth it has today. It was made up of families with kids who tolerated the Cub fans during the summer months. There were several bars on our block, and we lived on the second floor above a machine shop. Since none of the boys at school seemed interested in me, I would wait for the weekends and travel to see my old friends who had since moved to Lathrop Homes, the only integrated "projects" in the City of Chicago. We were told that Mayor Daley had insisted on a quota system for renting out the subsidized housing. It seemed safe enough for me to travel there most days.

HIGH SCHOOL ROMANCE

It was there at Lathop Homes that I met Raymond Jackson. He had arrived on the scene with his brother and his friends who were dating my friends at the time. He was the tallest and the toughest. Those attributes were attractive for me as I had sworn that I would never be victimized again in my life. I thought, What better protection for a fifteen-year-old girl but to have the toughest boyfriend in the neighborhood? This theory backfired on me when his toughness turned to violence against me.

My mom was still working six days a week. She had three teenagers and one pre-teen under her roof, and she looked totally exhausted all the time. She allowed Raymond to come and visit. By this time I had been expelled from Luther North for various reasons. I fell madly in love with the idea of being in love at fifteen with someone who promised to love me forever and to take care of me and protect me. I refused to return to high school, and by the time the truant officer got around to me, (since I was only fifteen and in Illinois at the time the rule was that you must attend high school until the age of sixteen) I discovered that I was pregnant. I was thrilled. I was thrilled to discover I was pregnant because even after all the drama of my childhood, I was still a true believer in Cinderella and living happily ever after.

FIFTEEN AND PREGNANT

I discovered I was pregnant right before my sixteenth birthday. I decided to wait to tell my mom because I believed she would take the news so much better if I was sixteen years old. I truly believed being sixteen would make the announcement easier for my mom. I was explaining this to one of my girlfriends on the telephone when my youngest sister, Donna, eavesdropped on my conversation. This invasion of my privacy was not hard to accomplish since the only telephone in the apartment was in the hallway. I had tried to stretch the telephone cord as far as I could so I could talk in the privacy of my bedroom, but, alas, Donna was determined to hear what I was whispering about on the phone. I had no idea that she had heard the entire plan and had passed this information on to my mom.

After dinner that night, my mom sat me down and asked me if all that had been told to her was, in fact, true. I was shocked. How dare my sister reveal this information, especially since she had obtained it by eavesdropping?! My mom was not amused with my righteous indignation. She stayed calm and asked me again, "is this, in fact, true?" I tried to explain that it was indeed true and I was only waiting to break the news in consideration of her feelings and how I truly believed she would have felt better about the whole situation had I just been allowed to turn sixteen first.

She assured me that no matter what age I was, a pregnancy outside of marriage was serious business. She would know. At this moment, I had no idea how blessed I was to have a mother who could relate to this situation and still speak lovingly and calmly to me. I also did not realize that this was God's plan and that my little baby was a gift from God. I was still in LaLa Land, dreaming about being Cinderella and waiting for my prince to come and carry me off on his white horse.

It wasn't until I was much older that a law professor told me that the way it looked to him was "that baby, your child, and the changes that came with being a mother, actually made you grow up and changed the course your life would take." Thank you, Neil, for such sage wisdom which I now know to be true.

My mom, who had seen so much in her life, said the following: "You can have the baby and keep it, you can have the baby and give it up for adoption, or you can have an abortion."

It was 1972, and abortion had gone from the back alley to the hospital. It still meant killing your baby but in a more sanitized "legal" fashion. Oh, my goodness, who would kill their own baby, I thought, even if it was legal? I would keep my baby. My mom agreed, and life went on.

Raymond decided he would drop out of high school and join the Marines with his cousin Ricky. The Viet Nam war was still going, and in order to avoid being sent directly to Viet Nam, he would join up so they could serve together in the "buddy plan." He promised he would come back and marry me after he completed boot camp and we would live happily ever after, traveling the world while he served in the Marines. I was sixteen, and I believed in fairy tales. My glass is always half full, what I can say?

MY NEW BEST FRIEND TARA

During my pregnancy, I tried to help out around the apartment as much as I could. My mom decided that I would keep the front bedroom and that my child and I could stay there as long as we liked and, of course, while Raymond was in the Marine Corps. By November of 1972, I had developed a strong addiction to the soap opera *All My Children*. I found it fascinating that young Tara Martin had also become pregnant and was about to go into labor right around Thanksgiving. I watched every day and believed this was as close to reality TV as I was going to get at sixteen. When Tara was in labor for almost forty-eight hours and in excruciating pain, I thought, "Yikes, is this what I have to look forward to?"

As it turned out, my water bag started to leak three weeks before my due date, and, thank God, my mom knew this was serious. We went to the hospital, and they decided to induce my labor. What does that mean, I wondered? Tara didn't have to go through this. Well, in 1973, inducing labor meant an enema. What the heck? This was extremely rude, I thought, but must be necessary. It must have been extremely uncomfortable for my baby as well because after only six hours I announced I was ready to deliver. "Oh no," the nurse said, "not after just six hours, this is your first child, and you are only sixteen so you really do not know what labor is or when you are really ready." She must have been watching Tara's forty-eight hour delivery, too, I thought, but I **knew** my baby was on her way. I screamed that if they did not take me to the delivery room, I would walk there myself because she was coming NOW. Sure enough, much to everyone's surprise I was almost fully dilated which meant NOW.

Less than fifteen minutes later the most beautiful little girl, Velma, was born, five pounds, ten ounces. When they tell you that as soon as you see your baby, all the pain goes away, they are telling you the truth. But I knew that from watching Tara's delivery.

MY MOM AND ME, A MOM

My mom decided we needed a crib for the baby. I thought the baby could just sleep with me, no joke. My mom went to Marshall Field's downtown and purchased the most beautiful canopy crib I had ever seen in my life. It was soft yellow with a lovely lace canopy. It must have cost a million dollars, I thought. Whatever it cost, it put her in deep debt. There is just no limit to my mother's love and grace. She was made in her Father's image, God the Father that is, not that earthly scoundrel that called himself her dad. If my mother had that much love and grace within her for us, just imagine the unlimited love and grace that flows from our Father in Heaven. I can make this connection now. I did not reach this conclusion at the age of sixteen, believe me. I was just trying to survive.

Now just because I tell you my mom was kind, do not think for a second that she was a pushover. She made it very clear. Velma was my child, and I was to be responsible for her. She reminded me that she was working six days a week, and so she could not be expected to get up in the middle of the night with my baby. Yes, Mom, no problem, I will be responsible, and you will not be awakened in the middle of the night for my baby, no way. For the first two weeks after Velma was born, I got up within seconds of her just making a peep.

My mom had also bought a small bassinet for Velma, and I kept it alongside my bed. The second she stirred, I was up. After about two weeks of this, my mom came to me and confided that she actually wanted to get up with Velma sometimes.

I did not have to be a Supermom, just a good mom with a lot of helpers. And helpers I had. My brother who did not believe in letting his niece cry for even a second and my two little sisters whom I eventually trusted to hold her and carry her around.

Raymond returned in March 1973 and announced that he wanted to get married but not for the reasons I thought.

I wanted to get married and complete the Cinderella story in my head. He wanted to get married so the government would have to pay an additional family allotment for me and his daughter. We went downtown and got married. That was that. Then to Ronny's Steak House for dinner. We celebrated the rest of the day. In the morning he had to return to the base.

Raymond's plan for collecting extra pay did not last long because he was dishonorably discharged in 1974. He had "issues" with authority and rules, and the United States Marine Corps is not the place for that.

When Raymond returned home, my mother decided it would be easier for her to find a smaller apartment and move out than for Raymond and I to do so. She moved with my sisters to a new apartment just four blocks away on Southport Avenue. It would seem like miles away soon enough.

My brother decided he would stay with Raymond, me, and Velma, and we would split the rent. I was still on track to be Cinderella. I might not have been in a castle yet, but I was living in a nice big heated apartment with my husband and my child. I was eighteen now, so I was definitely all grown up.

Raymond got a job as a grill-cook in a restaurant as

this is the only skill he had obtained in the Marine Corps. While the recruiter had told Raymond he could choose his own career; Raymond's career test indicated he would make a fine grill-cook. He did in fact work at this job until he was fired. He was able to collect unemployment, and that seemed to suit him just fine.

PRINCE CHARMING GOES BALLISTIC

Raymond resumed some old friendships with some females when he returned home. I came home one evening and found him very boldly talking on the phone, our phone, the hallway phone, in our apartment, to one of those female friends. I confronted him, as I believed I had a right to do, being married after all, and he went ballistic. This was the first time I had experienced his rage and anger. It never even entered my mind that he might become violent toward me. But he did. He slapped me in the face so hard I thought I literally saw stars. This was only the beginning. He slapped me and hit me again and again. He knocked me down to the floor. He had his leg drawn back to kick me in my face when my brother Keith walked in. Keith was shocked by the scene. He had never seen the violent side of Raymond. He promptly ordered Raymond to stop and to "get off of my sister." Raymond seemed stunned that my passive brother would intervene on my behalf and threatened to kick Keith's ass if he didn't butt out. But my brother did not believe in hitting girls, and he sure as hell was not going to stand around and watch me continue to get beat. So he calmly told Raymond, "That may be, bro, I might get my ass kicked, but you are going to get off of my sister now, one way or another or else."

To my surprise, Raymond walked away saying under his breath that he could kill my brother with his bare hands and that my brother was crazy. I was battered and bloody, but I was alive. Now this should have been enough for me to leave him and get a divorce and move on with my life. If you are familiar with domestic violence situations, then you know it did not take long for Raymond to convince me that this was entirely my fault. Even my hero of a brother confirmed that I had brought it on myself in the way that I spoken to my husband.

Imagine that. I question why my husband is talking on the phone to another girl. I get the crap beat out of me, and it is my fault? Okay, I'll go with that. So I forgave him that one. But secretly I was making plans to become independent so that I could take my daughter and leave.

The first step to independence was a job. I had even fewer skills than Raymond. I was a high school dropout.

I applied at the local Burger King a few blocks away from our apartment. To my surprise, I was hired immediately and started to work evenings. This work schedule suited Raymond just fine as he continued his extra marital affairs. My younger sisters, Donna and Darla, were perfectly happy to help out with the babysitting of little Velma. I had learned to keep my mouth shut when it came to Raymond and his ways. I simply wanted a way out.

Working at Burger King gave me enough money to pay my half of the rent and feed my daughter. I could not afford anything else, and Velma had developed asthma. It was 1976, and if you went to the doctor you either paid with cash or used a medical card from the government. I decided I needed to swallow my pride and seek out some help from the government. I did not want to be on welfare, nor was I looking for food stamps. I did need to get some way to pay for the doctor's bills, the emergency room visits, and her medicine. I made an appointment at the local welfare office hoping I could find some help with these medical issues.

I was greeted by a young hippie-type social worker, beard and all. I recognized a hippie when I saw one. I explained the situation to him and asked for a medical card for my daughter, a "green card" as they were known. He literally was taken aback at my limited request. "That's all you want," he said. "Yup, that's all I want. I have a job, and I just need help with the medical bills." He began to explain that in Illinois I was "entitled" to much more than that if I was separated from my husband and without his support. Well, I was going to be very shortly as I was still planning my escape. I had to be very careful and try to convince Raymond that he would be happier without me so that I did not risk another violent beating. I really wasn't going to count on my brother to rescue me the next time as he was heading off to the Air Force himself soon. I would be left to fend for myself. I was no match for a six-foot, two-inch ex Marine, especially one with a dishonorable discharge.

The social worker explained that if I was really on my own, I could quit my job at Burger King and stay home with my daughter until she was six years old. There was no requirement to work. I could stay home and receive food stamps and a medical card and a monthly check. Since no one in my family had ever been on welfare before, this concept was foreign to me. It was foreign and yet very interesting and certainly worth looking into. I discussed the idea with my girlfriend, Deborah, who had a few kids of her own and had also experienced a few domestic beatings. She agreed that I should pursue that route. Not only would I apply for welfare, food stamps, and the medical card, but I would also apply for an apartment in Lathrop Homes, the "projects" where I originally met Raymond. Then I could leave, be financially independent, be with Velma, and plan my life from there. And so I did.

I was accepted into the projects almost immediately because of the racial quota system in place. These were the only projects in Chicago that were to remain integrated at all costs. Being white gave me an advantage because there were openings in the apartments, and they needed more white families to make the quota. I was given a one-bedroom apartment on the third floor for $47 per month. Since I was receiving $216 a month, with food stamps, I was rich. Velma and I moved out, and I announced that I planned to get a divorce through legal aid. Raymond did not seem to mind the idea of being single again.

ON MY OWN
WITH VEL

A few months went by, and I decided I needed to get to church. I contacted a former teacher at Luther North High School, Mr. Hertzog, and asked for a referral to a church where Velma and I would be welcome. He sent us to St. James Lutheran Church in the Lincoln Park neighborhood. This where I met Pastor Degner and his wife Martha. The reality was, and unfortunately still is, that not all churches are as welcoming as others, and some are downright unwelcoming. Where would we find a church that would welcome a single mother and a little girl? Well, at St. James Lutheran, of course.

It was a blessing that Mr. Hertzog even remembered me from biology class since I tried to fly under the radar in most classes. I guess a student who gets expelled for hitting a teacher is hard to forget. I did not really hit a teacher. My sewing teacher kind of pushed me so I kind of pushed her back, just harder, I guess. She sent me to the principal's office where I discovered that they had a file with all my mistakes, including forged parent letters regarding unexcused absences and various other misdeeds. All these incidents together led to my expulsion. Okay, that's my story, and I am sticking to it. Needless to say, high school had not gone well. Sadly, nothing had gone very well for me since that night my father changed everything. Before that night I was an "E" student, and E stood for excellent. I had been double promoted from the second grade to the fourth grade. I loved school. But not after that night.

We joined St. James Lutheran Church Missouri Synod. It seemed like a good fit. They had a nice young pastor, and, after all, Mr. Hertzog had recommended it.

It didn't take long before Raymond realized we were really, really gone and that we were not coming back. Single life was not that much fun for Raymond, and he showed up on my door begging for another chance. My brother had joined the Air Force, and that left Raymond all by himself to pay the rent in our old apartment.

I knew I would lose my apartment and my welfare benefits if I actually really took Raymond back. I was able to convince him that he could not move in full time. He just kept coming around. Velma missed her dad. One visit led to another, and in January 1977 I found myself pregnant again with my second child.

Now, I had plans. I had decided to go back to school, and I had even decided where I was going. I had gotten a catalog from Loop City College, now known as Harold Washington College, and I was going to pursue law enforcement, now known as criminal justice, and I was going to start in September. Since I was on welfare, I could qualify for a grant to pay the tuition and books. I could go to school part time until Velma started school. That was the plan.

At this point, I was officially separated from a very violent crazy man and pregnant. I was raising my four-year-old daughter, living in the projects, and on welfare. I was not able to go back to school to even get my GED. I felt lost. I felt like I was going to lose my mind. I even thought of perhaps not having this child. Yes, I am ashamed to write this, but I did think about it. After all, abortion was legal. Even though I knew it meant actually killing my baby, I did think about it.

AND THEN THERE WAS SARAH

But God was with me. He knew how desperate I felt. Somehow He gave me the idea to call Pastor Degner to discuss my situation. I had not been to church in months and I was embarrassed to call him, but I remembered the bible story of the lost sheep and how happy the Shepherd was when he found the lost sheep. So I called him. After all, I was lost. To my delight, he came over the very next day. He came from the nice area of Lincoln Park to the desolate projects. He came to the dirty, dangerous, roach-infested projects to help me. Wow, he truly was a man of God, and his work had just begun.

What Would Jesus Do?

Pastor Degner knew what I was thinking even though I never had the strength to actually say the words out loud. He knew from my voice and the tears in my eyes as I told him my story. And yet, knowing my deep dark thoughts, he never once lectured me or tried to tell me what to do. He simply, with genuine love and compassion, told me the story of Sarah, his newborn daughter. He told me the story of how she was born and how much joy she had brought to him and his wife, Martha. He told me how she truly was a gift from God. He talked about how they did not think they were ready for a family but that God knew they were. They were blessed with Sarah.

God gave Pastor Degner just the right words to say. I found myself actually happy for the first time in weeks. I wanted this baby so very much; because of course she was as much of a gift as her sister. I would have this gift, and life would be okay because God does not make mistakes. But Pastor Degner was not just a man of wisdom when he spoke. He also realized the reality of my situation. He contacted the obstetrician who had delivered Sarah and asked the doctor to accept me as a patient right away so my prenatal care could begin immediately. She said yes. This was big, really big, because most doctors did not accept the green medical card, especially at Prentice Women's Hospital, the finest in the land. I would give birth at one of the finest hospitals in the state. Jesus was really taking care of us.

• • •

When Samantha was eight months old, I was eligible for a bigger apartment in the projects because with two kids, you get a two-bedroom. There was a vacancy, and I moved down the street to a two-bedroom row house. It was located in a courtyard with other buildings and some of my teenage friends who had had kids as well and had moved into Lathop Homes as well. Even though it was dominated by gang bangers, these were the kids I had grown up with. I did not see the danger inherent in living in the projects. I actually felt safer because I knew all the gang bangers so well.

Raymond floated in and out of our lives, each time more violent than the last. By the time Samantha turned one year old, I had returned to my original plan and enrolled at Loop College. They agreed to allow me to take college classes while studying for my GED. Since I had almost completed three good years at Luther North, the GED test came and went rather easily for me. I began to enjoy school and the law enforcement classes and set my sights on becoming a Chicago police officer. I had met a female juvenile officer in my youthful travels and thought she possessed the most power I had ever seen. Surely no man was going to abuse her. Yes, I thought, that is what I will become, a juvenile officer, just like her. In my life I formerly sought strength in others to protect me, and they had only turned that force back on me. I would have to protect myself.

While I was attending St. James Church with the children, Velma was actually enrolled in the Lutheran grade school. My relationship with God was basically reserved for Sunday mornings in church. There was no time for him throughout the week because I was too busy trying to stay alive. Raymond did not accept the divorce very well and kept trying to force his way back into our lives. We were living in the projects so his violent behavior did not really shock anyone. After all, it was the 1970s, and alcohol and marijuana flooded the projects. It seemed as though everyone there was just trying to survive.

SURVIVAL BECOMES MORE DIFFICULT

Raymond would not always take no for an answer. Sometimes when I refused to open the door, he would just kick it in. Once he would gain entry to my apartment, it was just a matter of time before my head would go through a window or I would find myself running out the back door to safety. Many times my neighbors opened their doors with seconds to spare for me to run inside to safety. When he realized that, even with his crazy violence, I was not going to take him back, he turned to more dastardly deeds. He was insanely jealous and was always accusing me of flirting with other men, even when I was pregnant. It had gotten so dangerous while I was pregnant with Samantha that I twice had to fake labor pains and request to be taken to the hospital in order to avoid a beating. This continued even after Samantha was born, and on one occasion, he picked up the children from the babysitter and took them to his sister's home.

He refused to return them without a promise of reconciliation. I would have done anything to get him to bring them home so I lied and agreed to his terms, just so he would bring the children home. Once they were safe, I refused to abide by his terms and actually called the police. Once the kids were returned safely, the police did not want any further involvement.

It was the 1970s. And so the violence increased. He would try anything to get me to let him back in. Nothing was beneath him, putting a gun to my head, setting the living room carpet on fire, and threatening to blow up the entire house. He was stalking me long before there was anti-stalking legislation. He tracked me to school one day and refused to leave until I agreed to see him. Since I was involved in the student government, the security officers knew who I was and expressed concern when this strange man showed up on campus. Raymond was a bully but no match for the college security guards, who escorted him off site in a most violent way. Now the stakes were really high. I was sure I would pay for the beating he endured by the college security. I knew it was only a matter of time before he caught up with me.

By 1981 I had gotten a work study job through college at a new company downtown across the street from the school. A new telephone company, MCI, needed part-time college students, and my counselor sent me for the interview. This was just the break I needed. Soon I was offered a full-time position with a salary of $12,000 dollars annually. That was more money than I had ever seen in my life. Certainly now we could leave the projects and have a better life. There was just one big problem. If we moved and Raymond followed us, we would never be free.

MAFIA VERSUS STREET THUGS—MAFIA WINS

I made the decision to contact my dad and ask him for help. My logic was simple. My dad was a bigger bully than Raymond and my dad was still heavily involved with union activities. He had a lot of union connections. Perhaps he could reason with Raymond and finally convince him to leave us alone forever.

My dad was thrilled that I needed his help. He had a conversation with Raymond, and we never heard from him again. I surmise the conversation involved my dad threatening to put cement boots on him and drop him in the Chicago River. Nevertheless, Who cares? I thought, he is gone.

The girls and I moved out of the projects just four blocks down Diversey Avenue, but the difference was like night and day. We rented an apartment on the second floor of a two flat. It came with a very nosy neighbor on the first floor, who monitored all our comings and goings. I felt like the girls were safe. They would have to be, with me working all day at MCI and going to school at night. By now I had transferred to Loyola University and was actually studying criminal justice courses. I still wanted to join the Chicago Police Department and even took the written and psychological tests for the position. Having passed both tests, I came face to face with reality: a city-wide freeze on hiring at the Chicago Police Department. This sucked. I was less than a year from graduation and had no job on the horizon.

One of my college professors, Dr. Bensinger, suggested I apply to law school. He thought I was smart enough and that I would make a good lawyer. Pursuing law school meant that I would have to work all day and go to school at night, four nights a week. When would I see my kids? How would they survive? I thank God for the people of St. James School and Church. They helped us along the way. I could not have done it without my mom and sisters and Uncle Truman who came over to make sure my kids ate dinner while I was gone. It is no wonder Velma and Samantha grew up to be strong independent woman, in the tradition of Bernice Fitzgerald. They were, through necessity, on their own most of the time.

Determined we would never return to the projects or have to rely on a man for support, I decided to apply to a few law schools. What the heck, I thought, I probably won't get accepted anyway. I did not know any lawyers, and no one in my immediate family had even gone to college. My mom had a high school education, and my dad dropped out of school. I decided to apply to three law schools. I applied to only three, because I really could not afford the application fees for a fourth choice. I applied to Loyola where I was an undergrad student, John Marshall, and IIT Chicago Kent College of Law. I was pleased when I was accepted at John Marshall. I was thrilled when I got the call from Kent that I had been accepted. "Okay, Lord, here goes."

LAW SCHOOL—WHAT WE GAVE AND WHAT WE GOT

The fall of 1984 marked the start of four years of work and school and totally missing a lot of my daughters' lives. Velma was eleven, and Samantha was seven. And yet, with angels to guide us we made it through. The first year of law school was exhausting. I worked all day and went to school four nights a week. This schedule got me home at 10:00 p.m. My last evening requirement was to make sure there was milk and cereal available for my girls the next morning. That was always a priority. I found that the grocery store was very peaceful around that time of night. Going up and down the grocery aisles all by myself cleared my head.

I did laundry at 5:00 a.m. across the street at the laundromat. I had to start work at 7:00 a.m. in order to get to school by 4:00 p.m.; this allowed me to study for two hours and be on time for classes which started at 6:00 p.m.

Yes, working full time at MCI, attending law school four nights a week, and interning at the state's attorney's office was a difficult schedule to maintain. My girls never really saw me too much. I told myself I was doing this for them. And that was the truth. But I was also doing it for me because if I had stopped to think about our life at that point I would have lost my mind. Sometimes being on autopilot with a huge goal at the finish line is enough to keep going.

Now, depending on who you are, you may be tempted to judge me. Was I neglecting my duties to raise my daughters? Let's review.

I was a mother who was determined to give my daughters a better life, better than the projects and welfare and food stamps. Could I have given them that without law school? Maybe. But I was determined to do what I thought was best for me and my girls. I was driven, I was obsessed with using my God given abilities to pull us out of poverty and in the process give them the luxury of choosing how they might direct the course of their lives.

My father had put a stop to my hopes and dreams. While my mother was very courageous and selfless in her decision to protect me by separating us as best she could from my abusive father, we lived in the direst poverty-stricken conditions for a long time. She worked nonstop just to keep us fed and safe. It was only natural that I would follow her lead.

God graced my first year of law school by allowing me the friendship with a "few good men" who didn't mind sharing their notes. They became very good, lifelong friends. My best friend, Lars, always told me that one of the reasons he did not mind sharing his notes was because he knew it was hard to manage raising a family while going to night school. He was married and had two young children. While he was at night school his wife was working very hard to take care of his kids. He could not even imagine going to law school at night after working all day if he did not have her love and support. So, really, I guess I should thank his wife Jan for the notes.

We did not have computers or laptops; we actually still used typewriters. We were the first class to actually have full-time use of the computer lab at Kent, but since I did not have one at home, what was the use of that?

Being in law school was difficult for me in a more in your face kind of way. There were also some very polished students there. It was challenging for me to understand the social positioning that went on. I was a smart, tough survivor, and I had earned my way into law school through hard work. Somehow I felt different from a lot of the other students. A few of them thought they were better than I, I'm sure. One even went as far as to tell me not to say "Hey, man" to the professor. I interpreted this as a direct slap against my streetwise upbringing. Nevertheless, I persevered. I was a good student, and that helped me in my interactions with the faculty. With the help of Professor Marc Kadish, I was given a chance to work in the law clinic. The experience of working in the law clinic was great. It was almost like being a real lawyer, and I cherished the thought. It helped build the confidence I needed to move into this more refined environment.

The next four years flew by, and in May 1988 I graduated. It was a time of great celebration for me, my girls, and my whole family. My mom knew we had to have a party. My mom got a big cake and made a lot of food, and a lot of my friends from law school and MCI came to celebrate this accomplishment.

Just when I was about to graduate from law school, my mom's husband died of a cerebral aneurysm. She had finally found a good decent man four years earlier, and he had just died.

PASSING THE BAR
AND LANDING A JOB

As stated, I worked at MCI all through law school. I had moved to the midnight shift a year before I graduated because I was offered an internship during the day at the state's attorney's office. I loved working in the prosecutor's office and hoped to get a job there after graduation. I needed to take and pass the bar exam to start this new career. I thought I could study better if the girls were not home, and I really needed to pass the bar exam. I accepted an offer to send my daughters to New Orleans to stay with our good friends Connie and Dave for a month in the summer. Thank God for friends and family.

By the way, during law school, the hiring freeze was lifted at the Chicago Police Department, and I was offered a job. Are you kidding me? I sat next to at least two police officers in law school, I was not about to go backward. That door was closed, or so I thought. I would never be on the police force now. Boy oh boy, Jesus must have gotten a good laugh at that attitude, for He knew what the future held.

The best laid plans of mice and men did not go so well; while my daughters were in New Orleans, I did not do much studying for the bar exam, and, alas, I received notice that I would need to take it again. I was devastated but nothing my girlfriends and a pitcher of margaritas wouldn't solve. The next time around, I studied for the bar exam with the girls at home, just like I did all the way through law school, and I passed with flying colors. Believe it or not, it was so easy and without any stress the second time. I just knew I had passed.

I was still working at my internship as a law clerk at the state's attorney's office when the news came that I had passed the bar exam. My judge, the Honorable Robert Boherick, called the first assistant at the state's attorney's office and asked him to hire me right away. My starting salary was $25,536, an amount I shall never forget.

MY REAL CAREER BEGINS

I was so excited to get this offer to work at the state's attorney's office. I was reaching a goal I had only hoped for. Unfortunately, the salary at the state's attorney's office was lower than the salary I was currently making at MCI. I thought, I cannot quit a job that paid more to take a job that paid less. So I did what any sensible mother would do; I decided to keep my midnight job at MCI and work at the prosecutor's office during the day.

My oldest daughter, Velma, was a senior in high school and was headed off to college. I needed to pay the bills and support my family. This arrangement would never have worked if my kids weren't so accustomed to fending for themselves. While I slept on the floor at home in the early evening, they would eat dinner and watch television.

My coworkers at MCI and the state's attorney's office were aware of my situation and did everything in their power to help me and cover for me when I needed "just a fifteen-minute nap." I will never be able to thank them enough for all they did and they know who they are. God continued to place people in my path who were good and kind. I was not always ready for all that was good and kind.

At the state's attorney's office I was sent off to the Appellate Division. It sounded very impressive but involved a lot of reading and research, neither of which I was too fond of. Since I was still working my midnight job, I found it hard to stay awake in the library. Each of us was required to write a minimum of three legal briefs per month. During my three-month stay I wrote nine briefs, you do the math.

When it was announced that a couple of people could volunteer to be transferred to the Traffic Division, I jumped at the chance. The Traffic Division was still located in a seedy building at 321 North LaSalle Street, having just barely survived the Graylord era. It was still quite the hustle and bustle courthouse with action one could have only imagined. I had a few good girlfriends there and a few good guy friends as well. I was still working the midnight job, and as soon as court was ended, I would race home for some evening nap time before having to go downtown to my other job at MCI. There were a few naps on the floor under a desk at MCI as well, and my good friends there are greatly appreciated. I stayed in Traffic Court for four months and learned how to litigate on a wing and a prayer. We would have only minutes to prepare for a traffic trial.

My next move was to the Bridgeview Courthouse in the southwest suburbs of Chicago. I had bargained my transfer in order to achieve my real goal which was to ultimately transfer to the Markham Courthouse. It was 1990, and all the action was in Markham, the Sixth Municipal District that handled the cases which arose out of the south suburbs of Chicago. I had been born and raised in Chicago, never having set foot in the south suburbs, let alone ever living out there. But to get to Markham, I was told I must accept an assignment at Bridgeview for three months first.

Bridgeview was as different from Markham as night is from day. The Bridgeview Courthouse, known as the Fifth Municipal District was a newer building. It was a nice clean, quiet building where the courtroom work would usually be completed by noon. This fit my schedule just fine, and thanks to my trial partner, John, an older more seasoned veteran in the office, I never brought my coat upstairs so the bosses never knew if I was coming or going.

In April of 1990 I finally got my wish and was transferred to the Markham Courthouse. When I arrived at Markham I was wearing a beautiful colorful flowered dress. This was my best attire. One of the more senior female state's attorneys pulled me off to the side and informed me that state's attorneys do not wear flowered dresses. She was senior to me, and there was tradition that you never bucked a senior attorney in the office. I felt like I was back in grade school again. But this was too much crap to take from anyone, and I promptly informed her I would wear what I had in my closet. Period. And besides, you are not the boss of me! My boss was Pat Quinn, the man that I had so loyally clerked for all through law school (Justice Pat Quinn of the Illinois Appellate Court, not the governor). He was the boss of Markham whom all feared and respected. He was the kind of boss that would walk on crushed glass for his people. He led by example, and he took no prisoners. He was the ultimate prosecutor's prosecutor, bar none. He was the kind of man who could recognize justice. He wanted the violent criminals locked up for life, and yet he had a compassionate side few rarely saw. He felt great pain for the victims of violent crimes. Less than a year later, he left Markham for a promotion at the Criminal Court of Cook County at 26th Street. I followed him and joined his team of Public Integrity Prosecutors. We were charged with investigation and prosecuting corrupt public officials including police officers. What a job! We investigated police officers accused of theft, sexual assault, and brutality. We all loved the police but hated dirty cops. I was the least experienced in the group but worked hard to try to achieve justice and not disappoint my fearless leader.

Eighteen months later I returned to Markham and was eventually assigned to the Felony Trial Division. The Felony Trial Division was the ultimate goal because this is where the most serious trials are handled. We had hundreds of cases in our courtroom ranging from bigamy to attempted murders. I worked in the courtroom of the Honorable Leo Holt. This man was an icon in Chicago. He had led by example throughout the Civil Rights era and was now sitting on the bench. He was not exactly the prosecutor's favorite because he had a passion for justice that put the rights of the defendant before all others. He soon became my favorite. He smoked cigarettes in his chambers and since I smoked as well, we got along just fine. And even though he had a different opinion on justice than I did at the time, I really loved being in his courtroom and grew to love him dearly. He became a good friend with much needed sage advice over the years.

My professional life seemed to be moving right along. I was still Karla Jackson, aka "Action Jackson" to most of the cops because I was always on their side. I could swear like a truck driver and also took no prisoners. I took advantage of my street upbringing and had the good fortune to learn from the mentoring of Pat Quinn. This combination made me a pretty tough cookie.

JUMPING FROM THE FRYING PAN TO THE FIRE

I t was while at Markham that I decided that it was time to actually consider my personal life again. I would start to date again. I bumped right into husband number two. Husband number two was the biracial equivalent of Eddie Haskel from the *Leave it to Beaver* show. Since my children were biracial I found him to be fascinating. When I discovered he was Lutheran as well, I mistakenly thought that this was a match made in heaven. He pretended to be very kind to my children and interested in their lives. Velma was at college, and Samantha was trying to survive the move from Chicago to the south suburbs. I was still looking for that Cinderella ending. I had not let go of "happily ever after."

He proposed on Valentine's Day, less than a year into our dating relationship with a heart shaped ring. I thought this was something out of a movie. We had a wedding in the Lutheran Church and large reception. I spent more time planning the wedding than thinking about what the marriage would be like. Big mistake. When I agreed to marry him, I made the incorrect assumption that he would never be abusive. I was a Cook County prosecutor and he was a police officer in a local town, but it did not take long before the abusive behavior began. And while he was never physically abusive, his mental and verbal abuse was horrendous. But the truth is that once you have endured physical and sexual abuse, especially as a child, it is hard to compare "mere" mental and verbal abuse in the beginning. I had never ever actually seen a good or normal relationship between a man and a woman up close. As the verbal and mental abuse became more and more frequent and painful, I figured that this would just have to do for the time being. I told myself to suck it up. I thought to myself, after all, it could be worse. It could always be worse, but I had no idea that it could be better.

REACHING FOR "THE BENCH"

With my girls growing up and my career going well, I decided to concentrate on my judicial aspirations. As most prosecutors in the 1990s, I believed that since my career as a prosecutor was going well, the next step was to run for judge, or to "sit on the bench." Most state's attorneys that I knew seemed to make good judges. Why not me?

My husband at the time supported my desire to run for judge for many reasons. He liked the idea of a major salary increase as he had dreams of his own. These dreams included a new car, a new house, a boat, a motorcycle, etc. These were things he could never afford on a small town police officer's salary. But if his wife was a judge? Well, suddenly acquiring these things were in the realm of possibility, and that would suit him just fine. A lot of the verbal and mental abuse had been about money and the limited salary of a State's Attorney versus a lawyer in a big law firm. He constantly complained about the material things we did not have and all the material things he wanted and needed.

I have never been attached to material things. The new brown coat in eighth grade was enough for me to see that. A coat does not a person make. I could never find, and still do not see, the pleasure in a purse that cost more than one hundred dollars or a dress that cost more than fifty bucks. I have some very good girlfriends now that do find joy in these things, and I am happy for them. It just is not for me. After all, Cinderella only owned one gown, but what a gown it was.

Given that I had decided to run for judge, I became politically active in the south suburbs. I naively believed that my good name and reputation ought to be enough to win an election. I was wrong.

A CASUAL FRIENDSHIP

My girls and I attended church on Sunday. I found a church nearby that seemed friendly enough. But I thought church was for Sunday, and since God was always going to be on my side, I did not really seek out a relationship with Him on more than a casual basis. I figured He knew me and I thought I knew Him and so if He wanted to get my attention, He knew where to find me. I realize this might sound arrogant. It really wasn't arrogance, rather, just laziness. I just didn't give our relationship too much thought or effort. Jesus was a good friend that I trusted, but one I really only turned to in times of need. At this point in my life I never even considered what God wanted of me, what God needed of me, or what His plans were for me. I took no responsibility for this relationship. I left it in His hands. I thought, He was God; if He wants me to know something, He will tell me.

There was no sense in looking for more things to do. My plate was full, or so I thought.

STARTING THE NEW YEAR WITH A BANG

O n December 31, 1993, I had a house full of people ringing in the New Year. And I was late. Yes, at thirty-seven years old with two almost grown daughters, my period was late. I decided to buy a home pregnancy testing kit from the drug store earlier in the day. I couldn't wait for everyone to leave so I could take the test.

As soon as the last person left, I made my way to the bathroom. Five minutes later, to my surprise and delight, I discovered I was pregnant. I was overjoyed. I was pregnant with a husband and a good job. This pregnancy would be different that the two before. I had good insurance through the county government and certainly everyone would be as happy as I was. Not so much.

My daughters were at first shocked that their thirty-seven-year-old mother was still having sex, but they seemed

genuinely happy to be getting a little brother or sister after all this time. My friends and coworkers at work were
happy for me as well.

My husband was another story. He had two sons from
a previous relationship and **did not** want any more kids.
His response, when I told him, was shocking and hurtful.
He went ballistic, screaming about how I was too old to
have a baby and how it would probably be one of those
"special" kids because of my age. This verbal tantrum continued well into the night and started up again each and
every day for the next six weeks. He was upset because we
had not planned for this, and he needed a lot more stuff;
he needed a new motorcycle, etc.

He continued to yell and fuss like a two-year-old. He
told me he did not want any part of this baby and that I
should get rid of it. I did not react well to his abuse.

First, I told him to go to hell. Secondly, I told him I was
going to have this baby come hell or high water, with or
without him.

A LONELY DRIVE

Unfortunately, that was not to be. In late February, when
I was twelve weeks pregnant, I drove myself to the Emer-

gency Room at a nearby hospital because I was spotting. While at the hospital I had a miscarriage.

Losing this baby was an extremely sad and traumatic experience for me. The grieving process was horrendous. I cried for days over the loss of my baby. My husband never shed a tear. He was convinced we should move on as though I was never even pregnant.

I went through the March primary with my name on the ballot and lost. After I lost the election, my husband announced that he needed some space. He decided he no longer wanted to be married, at least not to me. I thought we should at least seek some marital counseling through the church before we just called it quits. He reluctantly agreed. I found out later that all the while during counseling, he was seeing another woman, who eventually would become his next wife.

So much for counseling.

SPREADING THE NEWS

While working at the Markham Courthouse, I had many different assignments before reaching a Felony Courtroom. One of the most stressful and yet rewarding was to work the "crazy counter" and the courtroom assigned to it. This was known as Courtroom 101. This courtroom handled everything from "soup to nuts," literally. All the domestic violence cases were sent there, as well as neighbor disputes and retail thefts from the local Kmart. Not many attorneys liked this room, but for me, it gave me a chance to work with victims of domestic violence as well as just crazy cases. There was no special training for the attorneys assigned to this room, and domestic violence was not seen as a serious crime as it is today. In the 1970s and 80s, the police were still telling victims of domestic violence to leave their own homes or telling the abuser husbands to take a walk around the block and cool down. Most abusers never got arrested. Those that did get arrested figured out the system, and most often the charges were dropped. No one who had not walked in the shoes of the victim understood why she did not leave, and a lot of people did not even care. Even in the early 1990s, most people in law enforcement felt conflicted about arresting a husband for slapping his own wife. I contend that it really was not until the O.J. Simpson case occurred and shined a light on domestic violence that the country actually took notice.

While this courtroom had the most entertaining judges assigned to it, it was overwhelming and even depressing at times. Litigating neighbor disputes and retail thefts are not as challenging as they are frustrating when you see the same faces over and over again. But with the domestic violence cases, it could get pretty scary. I knew most times that the victims were in *real* danger, but without any evidence to support these fears, most charges were dropped. Having gone through many serious beatings myself, I knew the violence always escalated. I knew that the abusers were just using the honeymoon stage to make up with the victims so they could get the charges dropped. I knew the cycle of domestic violence all too well. But most women did not think I knew anything about what they were going through.

Things improved a little in the cases involving domestic violence when we prosecutors had the help of court advocates. A court advocate was a woman who worked for a local not-for-profit agency and helped victims navigate through the court proceedings. The advocate understood the cycle of violence that these victims were experiencing and knew what to say to the victims at a time when a lot of prosecutors did not. It was a step in the right direction, but it was not enough.

I decided that it might be helpful if I went semi-public with the story of domestic violence I had experienced at the hands of my first husband. I thought it might help other women to understand that it can happen to anyone. I wanted them to know that it was not their fault and that there was life after domestic violence, that they could escape it and survive it. I thought that if they knew that I had walked in their shoes that they would take my words more seriously when I said that it will only get more dangerous if you do not leave. At the very least, I thought I would have more credibility with the victims in my courtroom. Maybe they would not continue to be part of the revolving door known as Courtroom 101.

Although we had a few success stories, they were few and far between. Most memorable was the day I was working the counter when a woman and her sister and her infant daughter came in. The woman looked totally beat down emotionally and wanted to know what she could do to stop her husband from being abusive. He was a doctor in a nearby community, and although he had "pushed" her around over the years, he was now actually throwing things at her. This did not bother her too much at first, until he threw the baby monitor at her while she was breastfeeding her baby. The monitor almost hit the baby in the head. This was too much for her to bear. Her getting pushed around was one thing, but now the baby was in danger. Everything seemed to fall into place. We quickly sought out the on duty judge, and as luck would have it, we found one who would consider giving her an Emergency Order of Protection and Exclusive Possession to the Home. Imagine that, the abuser would have to leave the home and the victim and her children could stay. I saw this same woman about six months later, and I did not recognize her at first. She looked happy and alive. She had hired a lawyer and was taking charge of the situation in order to protect her children.

Although the police and the courts had advanced a little bit from the days when they used to tell the husband to take a walk around the block to cool off, there was still no dedicated police units for this crime, no specialized courtrooms or training for prosecutors. Although the advocates knew the cycle of violence, and the profile of a batterer, no one really cared to dedicate the time or the resources to this epidemic. Although our assigned judges were good about taking it as seriously as anyone else, we once had a substitute judge who actually suggested to the abusive husbands that "candy and flowers" always worked. I am not kidding. That is what he actually said in court. We were furious and it showed. In actuality, the judge could not have cared less what we thought. He said he was just kidding and ignored our rage.

This was the basic sentiment of the courts and the police in the south suburbs prior to 1994. This is not to say that no one was on our side, because that would not be true, but, basically, few understood the Profile of a Batterer. They did not know the Domestic Violence Cycle or the stages it involved. The South Suburban Family Shelter and the Crisis Center of South Suburbia were and still are great resources and are staffed by well-educated, underpaid staff who could probably double their salaries in the corporate world but choose this service instead. The staff at these shelters worked very hard to change the judicial system's understanding of domestic violence and helped make our community a safer place for families to live.

I knew I was privileged to work alongside these people and to be a part of this change.

WELCOME TO CHICAGO HEIGHTS

God put a lot of people in my path who helped me along the way all my life. I would like to think that I was placed in the path of others as well. One day in April 1994 a woman walked into the state's attorney's office in Markham and asked to speak to me. I had done an interview with a local newspaper the year before and had detailed my domestic violence survivor story. As this lady approached me, she looked scared to death. She looked as though she had not slept in weeks. It took all the courage she could muster to come to the courthouse because she was the wife of a Chicago Heights police officer. If she was seen going to the courthouse and talking to a state's attorney, her husband would go crazy. It was likely she would be seen because the Chicago Heights police were always at the courthouse and in the state's attorney's office. She was taking a big risk, but she was desperate.

She began to tell me her story, and I was horrified. Her husband had physically abused her for years, and the police had done nothing to stop him. Finally, he had been warned by the chief of police not to beat her any more. While his painful beatings had stopped, his abuse turned more devious and psychotic. His latest abuse had left her so unnerved that she decided to risk it all and ask me for help. She had read the news article and believed I was her last hope. His latest attacks included spitting in her face while he cleaned his guns. He sometimes held a gun to her head while verbally threatening her life. He had stopped beating her in areas of her body where it would leave marks that the outside world could see. This brave woman sat in front of me and told me that her husband only did these horrifying things on the weekend when the mayor's office and the courthouse were closed. She feared he was going to kill her and that it would be covered up by his friends on the job. Whether this was true or not, she certainly believed it.

What could I do to help her? I did not work on the weekends either. I decided to do what any self-respecting state's attorney would do. I gave her my home phone number and told her to call me if he tried it again. She could call me, and I would help her. Yup, I sure did. After all, I had no idea who her husband was, and I really did not care because I knew she needed help.

I grew up in the City of Chicago and knew nothing of the history of Chicago Heights and the Chicago Heights Police Department. So when this woman identified herself as the wife of a Chicago Heights Police Officer, the reality of the situation was lost on me for the moment. I knew that the Chicago Heights Police Department was not exactly domestic violence victim friendly. That was an understatement. In fact, the director of one of the south suburban domestic violence agencies had labeled Chicago Heights the worst city in the south suburbs for domestic violence victims. She had even gone as far as advising her clients to move out of Chicago Heights for their own safety because they had no trust in the police force to do the right thing when it came to domestic violence victims.

When I got home that evening I encountered my estranged husband who had stopped by to pick up some more of his clothing. I told him about my meeting with this woman as we still were able to chit-chat. He went nuts. "Are you crazy?" he said. Did I realize who this guy was and what he was capable of doing? He chastised me verbally for getting involved in "private matters." I suspected he simply did not want his name involved in this soon to be mess.

The weekend came and you guessed it, my phone rang. It was she, and her husband had started cleaning his guns again very close to her head.

I immediately advised her to call the police and to my surprise she responded that she had, and they were, in fact, right there in her home as we spoke. They had refused to do anything simply on her word, over his denial of the events.

"Oh, hell, no!" I said. "Let me speak to that police officer. I will get to the bottom of this." I announced that I was a Cook County state's attorney and that I expected him to treat this case like any other case and not give this police officer any special treatment. I warned that if anything happened to her as a result of his negligence, I would have his badge. No joke, that was what I said, and I meant every word. Little did I know that this event would go unnoticed like all the rest. The officer on the other end of the phone line was not impressed. While nothing was done that night to stop the abuse, I did what I thought was right, and that was all that mattered.

IMPRESSED WITH SUCCESS

I continued to stay busy working and trying to stay politically active. I had every intention of running again for a judgeship. After all, if at first you don't succeed, try, try, again. That was my motto.

God continued to place strong women in my life, and one such woman was Suzie. She was a prominent Republican woman in the community, and she was very active in her church. She invited me to attend a women's luncheon where she was the featured speaker. She gave a talk on hearing God's call. As I listened to her speak, I thought, "Wow, how powerful, how impressive, to be able to talk in front of all these people and share her story. I wondered to myself if I could ever do anything like that. She spoke about how God had let some doors close for her only so that He could lead her through new ones. She knew for sure that when one door closed, another one opened. We need to be willing and ready to walk through it. If we do, God will lead us where He wants us to go.

While I was extremely impressed with Suzie, I found myself thinking that this kind of sharing was only for certain people, people like Suzie, polished and pristine. What about people like me? Did I really think God had the time to keep up with all the doors that were closing around me? Especially since door #2 (aka marriage #2) was also about to slam shut.

A WINDOW OPENS

I was working through my election defeat and the ultimate failure of my second marriage. All the while, I was trying to care for my daughters and my elderly aunt who had moved to the south suburbs. My brother and I were trying to provide a roof over her head and her actual care as she was in a wheelchair because of a fall which literally broke her neck.

This aunt was the sister of my father. The same aunt who did not believe me as a child when I told my mother about the abuse perpetrated against me by her brother. The same aunt who continued to try to speak highly of him in my presence. With no husband or children, it fell to my brother and me to try to do the best we could to help her.

For a while my daughters took turns spending the night with my aunt as she insisted she could not be left alone. This did not last very long. My daughters were young adults, and although they volunteered to help as much as possible during the day, babysitting a spinster elderly great aunt at night was just not what they could handle for more than a few days. Even when she finally offered to pay them, they declined. No one could blame them; she was very demanding.

My sister Darla became aware of a family at her church that had fallen on hard times because of an unexpected injury and loss of employment. This led to foreclosure and bankruptcy for them. This was the spring of 1994, and most families had not experienced this kind of financial disaster. God turned their lemons into lemonade when my sister invited them to stay with my aunt. She approached them with a proposition she thought might benefit everyone. God had once again come to my rescue as He knew how hectic my life was about to become. Darla suggested that Ed and Chris move into my aunt's three-bedroom house free of charge in exchange for some care and companionship for my aunt. This was brilliant. They accepted immediately as they were living in a one-room basement apartment at the time. They had three children who adopted my aunt as their very own. They took her to church with them, and all was well for many years.

But Chris was brought into our lives to help me as well even though I did not realize it at that moment. She would end up being there for me in my time of desperation as my second marriage came crumbling down and my world was spinning out of control.

Coming face to face with losing an election, losing a child, and a failed marriage all within the same six months was very depressing. Chris was not into depression, nor was she going to allow her new friend to participate in any pity parties. She had been a drill sergeant in the US Army prior to marrying Ed and it showed. "You need to suck it up, my dear," she would say to me on a daily basis.

One fine day as I was visiting her and my aunt, she insisted that I accompany her to church for a Christian concert. I liked Christian music, and I listened to it on the car radio. It was also virtually impossible to say no to this woman, so along I went.

This was no Lutheran Church, and this music was not to be found in the old German hymnals. It was evangelical spirit filled Christian music at its best. There was clapping and singing and standing and waving and, oh, my goodness, this was not at all what I was used to doing in church. This was so foreign to me as we always sat so very still and quiet in church and never spoke unless spoken to first. We never jumped up and shouted "Amen" or anything like what was happening there. I could hear, "Yes, Lord, yes,

Lord," while hands were in the air, waving from side to side. This was real worship from real Christians who loved the Lord with all their heart and all their soul. I could feel Jesus in the worship. I had never seen anything like this in my life. I had come from the Missouri Synod Lutheran Church, where women did not even serve as ushers back in the day. Clapping and shouting and worshiping on your feet? Come on!!

I was overcome by joy. I made it a point to purchase the cassette tape of the music. (Yes, cassette tape, it was 1994, after all.) I played this music over and over again in my car for daily strength, and I fell in love with this brand of worship.

God knew He had to move me out of my comfort zone and allow me to step out of the church I had grown up in if I was ever to find my way home to the Catholic Church. I needed to step out of the boat and walk on the water with Him. I was able to gather strength from all of God's people that He set in my path in the south suburbs. God loves all His people and does not discriminate in heaven between denominations. I simply believe that the best way for me to truly serve my Lord and Savior is from within the Catholic Church. I shall explain. Please read on, my friends.

JULIE CONTINUES TO GIVE AND GIVE AND GIVE

My mother was still living in Chicago with my brother and his little boy. She was doing the best she could to care for her grandson whose mom had just died from breast cancer. Some days the south suburbs seemed so far away from Chicago as we were all doing our best to cope with daily drama.

THE BIG DOOR OPENS, WILL I WALK THROUGH IT?

I was still working as an assistant state's attorney in the felony courts, and was trying to resume some sense of normalcy when out of the blue I received a call from a police detective in Chicago Heights. He was a friend of mine and yet I was surprised to hear from him. I had worked with him and another detective on a youth program in Chicago Heights, but this call was unrelated to that.

He informed me that the mayor of Chicago Heights would like to meet with me. I was well known to the police officers and detectives in Chicago Heights as I had prosecuted their cases in their courtroom for many years and had worked closely with them on the felony review of the most serious cases. They had originally given me the nickname of "Action Jackson," and that name had stuck with me. I was known as a no-nonsense prosecutor who always backed the police, as long as they were trying to do the right thing. I was not offended by their rough language which at times I used myself. The mayor had only met me for a minute at a youth summit at City Hall, so I assumed he wanted to speak to me about a youth program. I had the faith and confidence of several detectives, and I assumed the mayor trusted them and their judgment as well.

The mayor and I met at a restaurant for our discussion. He informed me that a few of the detectives that he did, in fact, trust had spoken very highly of me and my professional ability. He knew all about my career especially my tenure in the Public Integrity Unit at the state's attorney's office, and he was impressed with my credentials.

I thought to myself, okay, sure, he was impressed, now, what did he want? Did he want me to serve on a committee? Did he want my professional opinion on gangs and drugs?

Whatever he wanted, I would surely do since he seemed so kind and I was sure if I helped him out professionally, it would help me in the next election. I was in no way prepared for the next part of the meeting. The mayor explained that the current chief of police was planning to retire soon, and they would need to find a new one to take his place. I instantly thought he was asking me to serve on a search committee for the new chief and maybe even help with the interviews of any future prospects. Before he could go any further I immediately responded that I would do what I could to help them and I would be honored to serve on a search committee. No, that was not what he had in mind. He stated, "Well actually, I was wondering Karla, if you would consider becoming the next chief of police?"

What??????????????????? Oh, come on, God, what is going on here? Certainly this is a joke right out of heaven for goodness' sake. I had always believed that God had a great sense of humor, but this? This was like being on *Candid Camera* or something.

Where had this come from? I had never gone to the police academy as I thought that door closed many years earlier. I was a lawyer, a state's attorney and besides there had never been a female police chief in all of Cook County and only a few in some small towns throughout the country.

The mayor told me that he had read about a New York prosecutor who had become the police chief of a small town, and he had been impressed with the article. He also wanted an outsider as some of the former police administration had gone to jail for corruption charges and he wanted to make a clean start and give the men on the force some new leadership. He wanted to restore the good name of the police department and its officers. He wanted them to be able to put the past behind them. He wanted new ideas for community policing and other programs that would help the citizens of Chicago Heights.

To say I was stunned would be an understatement. I quickly tried to come up with reasons why this would not work. I am not sure why but I gave him what I thought were three very respectable stumbling blocks to this offer. First, I did not live in Chicago Heights, and I knew they had a residency requirement. He politely said they would waive that requirement for two years. Secondly, I was a felony attorney with a very promising career in the state's attorney's office so I would need to make at least $75,000 dollars a year to change careers midstream at thirty-seven years old. "Not a problem," he responded. Third, I would require a contract guaranteeing my employment and/or compensation for at least two years. "Done," he said.

I was out of reasons not to accept this job offer, so I said, "Yes, thank you very much." We shook hands, and the deal was done. Of course, it would require approval from the city council. The council members trusted the mayor and his judgment and voted to approve my appointment.

I drove home thinking that God was about to send me into the lion's den as I knew of the previous corruption that had transpired in the city and the police department. The former mayor, former police commissioner, and several police officers had been indicted by the federal government and were awaiting trial. As I drove home I questioned God but trusted Him all in the same prayer. I confided in my pastor and looked for direction as I did not want to mistake this for a calling if it wasn't. My pastor agreed, it looked like a calling to him as well. Great, with the pastor on board, there was no wiggle room.

The next day my estranged husband stopped by the house to pick up some more clothes, and I told him about my meeting with the mayor. Oh, my goodness, it was as though I had spit in his face. He was outraged that I was offered the position and ranted and raged about life not being fair. So much for his support. Within minutes he began to realize that this new position might be vicariously beneficial to him, and so he decided not to file the divorce papers just yet. He would try to stick around for a large marital settlement as he always hinted he was due alimony. We would stay married on paper for now.

THEY NEVER EXPECTED A GIRL

There were only two people in the police department that knew of this offer, and I could only talk to them about the upcoming transition. I contacted a girlfriend whose law firm concentrated on municipal contracts, and together we drafted an ironclad contract that would protect me financially for two years. When I gave my notice at the state's attorney's office, the rumors began to fly at the Chicago Heights Police Department that a state's attorney was coming to be the new chief of police. As to which state's attorney, they began to guess. Several names were thrown about, but mine never came up. They narrowed it down to the top three, all guys, and the waiting began.

My appointment was announced in mid July 1994, and I began my transition period the next day. This was a big thing in the Chicagoland area because I was the first female police chief in Cook County. This generated a lot of press coverage and gave me the opportunity to help the department regain their reputation, a reputation that had been tarnished very badly by a few bad apples.

If this was a calling, then I had better have the nerve to accept it. As Suzie had said at that prayer meeting, when one door closes and God opens another, He will give you the courage to walk through it.

A NEW CHIEF IN TOWN

All of us thought it would be a good idea if I had a two-week period with the outgoing chief of police in order to make a smooth transition. Smooth it was not. During this time, I happened to hear a conversation between my new secretary and one of the sergeants. As I walked closer to her office, I could hear him actually screaming at her at the top of his lungs. All this for a scheduling error that had been made by either me or her, still not sure.

"Oh, hell no," I thought out loud. If anyone was going to be yelling and screaming, it was going to be me, and certainly not at my secretary.

I walked into my secretary's office and got directly in this officer's face. I began my own tirade on how things were going to change and change on August 1 when I officially took over as chief. I verbally chastised him with words that would have made a truck driver proud. He certainly did not expect them coming out of a size eight, 135-pound female.

Word spread like wildfire that I meant business. The outgoing chief chuckled and said, "Kid, you are going to be just fine. I was worried about you at first, but I think you are going to be all right." We continued the transitional period, and he gave me a lot to think about. My time to take over was just around the corner.

The officers soon learned I was not a pushover by any means, and that where Action Jackson left off, the new chief began. They knew I took this assignment seriously. But this was a tough crowd, an all-male tough crowd. Word spread that I intended to "really" be the chief of police and not spend my days getting manicures as was the initial rumor. If I was going to be paid to be chief, then I was going to be chief, period.

It helped that the mayor and I were on the same page. We agreed about the direction of the police department and the changes that had to be made. He was a good Christian man who wanted the city and the department to shine. He believed in the concept of community policing, professional training, and the idea of internal affairs, as did I, and we began the task of reorganization of the department that had suffered in the press from the past deeds of the former deputy chief, who was now in the custody of the federal government.

My secretary was invaluable. Like the Citibank commercial says, "Priceless." I depended on her knowledge and the advice of a few trusted souls within the department.

I still attended church on Sunday but running the police department was a big job, 24/7. I was sure God understood how busy I was.

POLITICS 101

Within the first year, our city had a mayoral election, and my mayor decided not to seek re-election. I really did not see how this would affect me; after all, I had a two-year contract. I was confident his successor would keep me on through the time I had agreed to. The contract was very well written; after all, I was still a lawyer, and I was sure no one would want to see me go so soon. I got a little concerned though, when the man I campaigned for was not elected. Politics 101: If your candidate loses, you are usually out the door. I had not taken Politics 101 yet, but I was about to get a crash course.

My second husband had announced he was leaving our marriage for good, and he suggested we get a quiet divorce. He had already moved out of our home, for the most part, and it sounded like a good idea to me. Little did I know that he was already spending a lot of time with the woman who would be his next wife. She was eighteen. I was almost forty. Nevertheless, we decided to go our own ways but not publicly just yet. We both got attorneys and began the tedious process of separating our lives. I confided in my secretary and a trusted detective. While we were trying to work out the financial details, my soon-to-be-ex-husband decided he would need alimony. This delayed the divorce and eventually turned into an attempt to coerce it out of me. I was not to be blackmailed, period.

As the news of my pending divorce became public, I talked a lot with my family and friends about my future. All thought I would be better off without him. Also, by this time, the friendship I had with my most trusted detective, Joe, had developed into a loving relationship. I felt a love for him that I thought I would never experience. Joe was also dealing with a divorce situation. We tried to be discreet about our relationship given that we worked together and we were both very private people.

My soon-to-be-ex-husband had other plans the minute he heard about my new romance. In an attempt to convince me to concede to his alimony demands, "so that he could continue to live in the style to which he was accustomed," he quickly spread the news throughout the community after threatening to ruin me and my career. He did neither. It was an embarrassing situation at worst. In the end, he was not awarded alimony. He was able to stall the divorce until 1996 and make my lawyers and me miserable.

The police department continued to advance professionally, and to everyone's surprise, the new mayor kept me on as chief through the end of my contract. He, too, was a good Christian man and an attorney. Of course, he did offer to buy out my contract, but I asked to stay and earn the remainder of my salary as I did not want to leave with so much yet to do at the department. I had some very good friends in the legal community that went to bat for me and spoke up for my job. Thanks to everyone who had faith in me.

When my contract ended, the mayor created a new position of superintendent of police and promoted me at the same time. This would give me more time to concentrate on administrative issues, legal issues, and grant writing. This would also put a layer of separation within the department so that a new chief of police could run the day to day operations.

We had grown from a department with seventy-four officers in general to a larger force with ninety-eight sworn positions which had become very specialized in their training and assignments. We had expanded the DARE (drug awareness and resistance education) program to include the first and second graders at all our schools, several community policing outposts, the largest K-9 (canine) unit in the south suburbs, and specialized domestic violence training.

By 1998 no one noticed when Joe and I finally wed and began a new life together in Chicago Heights. Joe adopted my younger daughter Samantha and gave her the Fiaoni name. This completed her dream of having a dad and an Italian last name, two things which she had wanted ever since she saw the movie *The Bronx Tale*. I became stepmother to Joe's son and daughter. Since I had only had girls myself, it was such a delight to have little Joey around. He was such a sweet little boy, and we all adored him. My older daughter had moved out of state to pursue her career in telecommunications and with both of my girls "all grown up," I threw myself into my work, particularly the grant work that had developed. I was in the right place at the right time and no coincidence, I was sure. I always believed that everything happens for a reason, and I certainly believed that God was in charge and that He would care for my every need.

As superintendent, I began to pursue federal and state grant money for police departments and the community at large. I stumbled upon a grant proposal request, an RFP, as they were called, that specifically outlined the need for Grants to Encourage Arrest Policies in Police Departments nationwide. I couldn't have been more stunned. This is what I was waiting for, this was why I was here, I thought to myself, for such a time as this; when domestic violence agencies had been advising their clients that Chicago Heights might not be safe for them, this grant work, this opportunity would spotlight domestic violence and give our department a chance to take the lead in this developing area of law enforcement. I would write the grant and the city of Chicago Heights would eventually be granted millions of dollars in program assistance. Once we were awarded the grant funding, it became increasingly clear that I was destined to run the program as it came out of my mind and soul, but, especially, it had come from my heart. This new domestic violence program would be an example to others on how all facets involved must come together to try to keep the victims of domestic violence safe in our community.

I became the director of the unit and we had several detectives and court advocates who joined me in our new office, two blocks from the central police station.

We considered ourselves to be a "one-stop shop" for those who found themselves on the receiving end of domestic violence and it soon became clear that we were not a team to be messed with, since the grant funding allowed us the time and effort to concentrate on these cases alone and since the police and the courts and the advocates were all working together. We saved many a victim from the cycle of violence during those years.

Since our domestic violence detectives were focused on our mission, the word went out through the community and the reports of domestic violence skyrocketed. Since many in the city council did not understand the epidemic of family violence nor accept the concept of underreporting which was widespread, the accusations came fast and furious that we had actually caused the increase of domestic violence. They did not want to believe that this violence had been going on for years and was not being reported. Headlines showed an increase of police reports alleging domestic violence up over 100 percent. It took a lot of explaining to finally get them to see the difference between statistical data that go unreported and the real violence that exists in the homes of all communities.

Our detectives executed search warrants in an attempt to obtain evidence against sexual predators that were victimizing young children in their homes, and we began a nationwide campaign to shine a light on this epidemic of family violence. I can truly say that of all the grants written during my tenure, the domestic violence grants were the ones I was the most proud of. After all, the need was great, and our hearts and minds were willing to do the hard work.

I WANTED IT STILL

N ow I still thought that I was destined to be a part of the judicial system so I unsuccessfully placed my name on the ballot time and time again. I suppose if God wanted me to be a judge at any given time, I would have won one of those races. Still, I wanted it.

I got very involved with the feminists in Illinois and even worked with them quite seriously. I thought we had a lot in common. I was against domestic violence. They were against domestic violence. I was for equal pay in the work place. They were for equal pay in the work place. I was still worried about women getting back alley abortions if abortions were not legal. So were they concerned. I held my pro-choice views in high esteem, even though deep down inside I knew that an abortion ended the life of a child, each and every time, and no question about that. I tried to buy into the "fetus" versus "baby" theory and the

123

"it's only tissue" justification. But, after personally experiencing my own miscarriage, I had nightmares about all the aborted "fetuses" in heaven with the child I had lost.

Out came the coping skills I had learned as a child in order to tame the dream keeper. I began to think about these thoughts and these babies during the day.

My time at the police department in Chicago Heights was coming to an end as we were transitioning the Domestic Violence Unit back into the mainstream of the police department. Grants never last forever, and it was time for me to return to the world of lawyering. I was encouraged by a close friend to try private practice. I was blessed to become friends with a very successful attorney with a big office in downtown Chicago who was willing to help me get started doing just that. Not only was he a very successful lawyer, but he was in politics as well. The political bug continued to bite at me and I found myself running for office again in 2002. But this was not just any office. This was for a seat on the Cook County Board of Commissioners. Wow, I thought I could do so much good and help so many woman and children if I were elected.

This process brought great scrutiny from many groups, one of which claimed to represent women on both the national and local level. They had a Political Action Committee with many members whom I knew. I considered these people my friends. I was wrong.

I also knew that if I were to get the endorsement of these organizations it would mean sure success. They always raised a lot of money and sent massive mailings out for their candidate. I knew the process for endorsement. I knew it too well. I had to answer their questionnaires correctly, and then surely I would get their backing. I was one of them or so I thought.

I obtained the questionnaire and began to fill it out. As I was reading through a questionnaire from an organization that claimed to represent women, I was stunned. This questionnaire started off with all the usual stuff, "Are you pro-choice?" Sure, okay, I thought, yes I was. But, by the time I got halfway down the page, answering question after question about invasive procedures, I discovered that if I wanted their support, generally being pro-choice was not good enough. You had to be "all in" as they say in Texas hold'em.

If I wanted their support I would have to agree that a woman had a right to "choose" an abortion at ANY point in her pregnancy.

What?

Even if she was in her third trimester. Even for any reason. Even if the "fetus/baby" were viable outside the womb, according to this questionnaire, she would have the "right" to an abortion.

I felt sick to my stomach. Even I knew that this "fetus" was really a baby, an actual human being. Even I knew that it requires ending the life of a baby when a woman has an abortion.

Oh, my goodness, if I wanted their support, I would have to agree with this. I would have to agree that it was okay to kill a baby at anytime for any reason as long as it remained in its mother's womb. Period.

The correct answers actually came with the question-naire so there would be no misunderstanding, if that can be believed.

Well, I was a feminist, I thought, but not a femi-nazi. I could not fill out this questionnaire the way they wanted. I could not sign it and pretend to believe these horrible ideas. So I did what any respectable human being would do. I refused to fill it out. Now I could have filled it out and expressed my concern for those babies being aborted, but I was not that brave. Not yet anyway. I knew refusing to correctly complete this questionnaire would mean my election attempts would probably fail.

There was another woman in the race, and she had gotten all the questions "right" and had gotten their support and their money and their mailers. I was told later by a close friend who was at the endorsement meeting that I was briefly considered but quickly shot down because I had failed to complete and return the questionnaire.

Oh, I had failed to complete it all right. I did not agree with them. But at that point in my life I still did not have the courage to stand up or even speak up for the unborn. What a chicken shit, I am, I thought.

What was God thinking as He watched my struggle?

I think God was thinking of new ways to strengthen my faith and give me courage.

So what was holding me back? Why was I still being quiet about this kind of murder? My head still held vivid memories of my mother's dear friend who almost lost her life because of a back alley abortion. I babysat and cared for her children for weeks while she was in the hospital and then later as she recovered at home from this botched back alley abortion. It made me so angry that this good woman almost died because she had felt like she was so desperate and there was no "safe" place for her to go. I incorrectly made the leap that if abortion was legal, it would be safe. This is not true, but at the time it seemed to make sense.

I wanted it to make sense so I would not have to confront the truth, the truth that no abortion is safe, not for the mother and certainly not for the baby about to be killed.

I did not like abortion, but I still felt like if a woman "had" to get one, there should be a safe place for her to go. (A safe place for her to go and kill her baby, and no safe place for the baby.) Now that I put this into words, it sounds so stupid and irrational.

But I was not quite ready to move either way, so I stayed in the middle. I thought I could stay there forever, but I was about to find out that you cannot serve two masters. I mean you really, really cannot serve two masters.

GOD SENDS IN HIS BULLDOG MARY

I was working very hard to get my law practice off the ground and going through the motions of everyday life. My girls were all grown up, and my husband was busy working most of the time as he had two younger children to provide for. I spent a lot of time working on various domestic violence projects and served on various boards. But mostly I was contributing my time outside of work as a speaker on a Domestic Violence Prevention Program being used in some area high schools. I had become friends with Mary, a woman who was helping with the administrative tasks of this program. We would occasionally meet to discuss the trainings over a cup of coffee. We would work on the lesson plans and the strategy for expanding the domestic violence prevention programs. We had been very successful doing the trainings in Chicago area schools and were about to move the program into other states across the country.

Mary set up what I thought was to be a typical strategy session over coffee. I think God had other plans.

Mary was Catholic, an Irish Catholic at that. She knew I was a Christian and she knew I was well-respected for my work in the domestic violence community. She had seen me work, and she had heard me speak on many occasions to many groups. She had read all the articles that had been done on me and my career.

She also knew I considered myself pro-choice.

Mary could not understand how I could be Christian and pro-choice. She felt this was a contradiction. We had worked together for a few years, and one day as we continued our work promoting our domestic violence prevention program, she began to question me about my beliefs. At first I found her annoying, and tried to avoid the subject.

Yes, Mary, it is difficult to be a Christian and still think a woman should have a right to kill her own baby but, hey, a lot of things are difficult, I thought as she continued to talk nonstop about this nonsense. What did this have to do with domestic violence prevention anyway? And by the way, it is none of your business so just butt out of my head would you please. Those were my thoughts.

At first I tried to be polite, as we had friends in common and I did not want her to think I was really the wicked witch of the west. As I tried to be polite in my response to her attempts to discuss this obvious conflict within me, I was getting angry with her. And as she persisted, I got nasty. Who the hell did she think she was anyway, questioning me, judging me? Just stop bugging me, please. In hindsight, I know that she was sent by God to get me to see into His heart. It was not the easiest assignment Mary had ever received from God and I am sure she probably questioned, why her?

As our friendship progressed, I had seen an article in a local newspaper describing a Christian shelter for pregnant woman who needed help to carry their babies to term. Any pregnant woman who needed a roof over her head and a meal and a warm bed while she carried her precious baby in her womb was welcome. Their goal is to keep these babies alive and also help them see that God loves them and has a plan for them and their children. I knew when I saw the article that I needed to get involved with this home in some way. I shared the article with Mary and asked her to help me in this endeavor.

We went to visit this place and met with the staff. We shared our ideas on how we might help, and they gave us a tour and a talk on their mission and their programs. I was sure if my mom's friend had had a place like this to go she would have been safe. I wanted to make sure that every woman had a place to go with her baby during a crisis pregnancy, and Mary and I continued to plan on how we could help them.

During this time, Mary continued to inquire as to my devotion to the pregnancy home and my continued pro-choice stance. She would bring this up at every coffee meeting and toward the end and I finally gave in and agreed to explain but only over a margarita.

Coffee would not do for this conversation.

MY IRISH FRIEND AND A MEXICAN RESTAURANT

Mary and I agreed to have dinner at a Mexican restaurant so I could have a few margaritas which I felt I needed if I was ever to explain to Mary once and for all how I was still pro-choice when it came to abortion. We were going to put this to bed once and for all, and I needed some tequila to do it.

As only God could have orchestrated, and to my surprise, I was not as hostile about the subject as I thought

I would be. This was the beginning of my realization of what my being pro-choice really meant. Now I was not stupid; I just wanted to believe the "it's only tissue" argument. We tend to believe what we want to believe.

Mary and I had gotten to know each other pretty well by now, and we had built up some trust between us. I knew she thought highly of me and my work. I knew she was a good egg. But why did she always have to talk about this abortion issue?

So when she asked me again why I was so adamant about this issue, I began to describe the events that led up to my mother's friend and her back alley abortion. The back alley abortion that almost killed her and almost left her other five children without a mom. Let me tell you, I did not like being backed up against a wall, forced to defend my indefensible position. I did not like it not one little bit.

Mary's simple question was, "Why would you advocate for a woman to have a choice to kill her child?"

Oh, sure, when you put it in those terms. My response was that the woman in my story was dammed if she kept the baby and dammed if she killed it through an abortion. What had pissed me off so badly was that the only option my mom's friend had was so Neanderthal, so crude, she almost bled to death. I thought if I could fight for women's rights. then women would have safe places to go and get good health care if they felt forced to have an abortion. I felt that women in crisis needed a better choice than a back alley.

As I was trying to explain my point of view to Mary to end this once and for all, she pushed back and said, "But Karla, there are places where women can go today. There are safe places they can go if they feel this is their only option. Maybe this was not the case thirty years ago when your mom's friend was in need, but there is a place for them to go like the home we just visited and many others. People like you have fought very hard to help women get the help they need in the courts. You do not need to fight this battle. It is done. You can help them make a healthy decision they can live with."

Easy for you to say, I thought. But actually it wasn't easy for her to say. She was not exactly the pushy type of girl and I was not one to be pushed. But God had given her a mission and had placed it on her heart and she was not about to back away now.

After our margarita meeting, we continued to meet, and I soon discovered that God was nowhere done with me. He had only just begun to open my eyes to what He wanted me to see.

AN INTERESTING RIDE

In December of 2004 our entire family with all four of the kids went on a Christmas vacation to Disney World. My husband and I could finally afford to take them all on a vacation.

They went on every ride imaginable, including Tower of Terror, as they loved fast roller coasters and all the upside down fast rides. I just sat on the bench holding all the purses and wallets as those kinds of rides were not my cup of tea. It was great fun just to get away and spend some time with the family. When we returned home after a week, things were about to get really interesting.

Through all the trials and tribulations, I never really thought of myself as a great mother. But given the circumstances, I did the best that I could do at the time. I knew I did, so I really did not have many regrets. As the lead character in the movie *ZOA* says, "If I could have done better, I would have done better…I could not have done any better as I did the best I could at the time."

Nevertheless, in early January 2005, my daughter Samantha, now twenty-eight years old, began to have feelings of sadness and experience mood changes. For three days in a row she found herself in tears for no obvious reason. After she missed a few days of work because of these unexpected and unexplained emotions, I suggested she see a psychiatrist. Yes, that's right, the first thing that came to mind was that this must be a result of my poor parenting skills and she must be in need of professional help if she was not able to just suck it up and go to work. Well, thank God, her girlfriends had another theory. They suggested she take a pregnancy test.

This had never occurred to me as both my daughters had previously announced they would be pursuing a career and marriage prior to any pregnancies, and I took them at their word. I had forgotten that God was in charge of when His children arrive on this earth, not us.

Soon thereafter, Samantha announced that she was in fact, not crazy but pregnant which accounted for all her emotional ups and downs because of her changing hormones.

I was going to be a grandmother. This was a dream

come true. This was better than being Cinderella, better than winning an election, better than anything.

Oh, Happy Day. I decided that Toys R Us could not wait, and neither could I. I began shopping for this grandchild who was only eight weeks old and still very comfortably in his mother's womb. Since we did not know whether it was a boy or a girl, I bought two of everything, pink and blue and every color in between. I spent thousands of dollars in record time on toys and clothes and anything else I could get my hands on. My car was stuffed to the brim with stuff. No room for anyone else, just me and my stuff.

It was on the way home I heard a voice deep down inside, deeper than I had ever heard. I did not know who was talking to me, but I thought it was supernatural because there was no one else in my car and the radio was off.

Voice: "Hmm, your daughter is pregnant, I wonder what she will decide to do?"

Me: "What?"

Voice: "I wonder what she will decide to do?"

Me: "What do you mean?" I asked of this voice.

Voice: "I wonder if she will have this baby or choose an abortion?"

Me: "Are you crazy?" I began to shout at this voice.

Me: "Abortion? What the hell are you talking about? This is my grandchild we are talking about."

Voice: "Well, you are the one who is always saying that a woman should have a choice, and after all, she is only eight weeks pregnant and you are the one who says it is just tissue at this stage, right? It is her choice, right? After all, this may not be convenient for her."

Me: "Okay now, I have had it with you whoever you are. This is my grandchild. Of course she will have it. So just shut up. Conversation over. Goodbye."

Now I was pissed off big time but admittedly getting a bit concerned. Not because I was hearing voices and that someone in heaven was taking to me. No, I was getting pissed off because they had the nerve to even suggest that my daughter would consider an abortion. Then I started getting scared. Oh, my goodness, what if He was right, what if this was not convenient for her, after all, she was still pursuing her education and her career.

I quickly drove home and called my daughter and tried to gently ask her the question without revealing how scared I was given this conversation in my car. How does one tactfully ask one's daughter if she is planning to kill her baby? To my delight Samantha told me, "Of course I am going to have this baby. It is a blessing from God."

Okay, okay, thank you Lord Jesus, but if you already knew that, why the heck did I just go through hell and back? And then He said: ***"Isn't every baby I send to earth someone's grandchild?"***

Okay, wow, I see your point, you must be God, and I am sorry that I ever got involved with the pro-choice movement, but come on, I have waited so long to be a grandmother and now you want to screw with my head over this? Is that really fair? I have been a good Christian, well, I have been a fair to moderately good Christian, well, okay, I am not that bad, right? And anyway Lord, you love sinners, so here I am.

THE BOOKS

Right around this same time my girlfriend Mary, yes, you guessed it, my Irish Catholic girlfriend was trying to get me to read some books that had been written by a Catholic woman named Anne, a lay apostle.

I am not Catholic, come on, Mary, I remember thinking, could you just leave me alone, please? And of course, the answer was no.

She gave me a set of four books from a series known as the Volumes. She asked me to read them, please, she said. Oh sure, but I was very busy, and again, I was not Catholic. But not wanting to seem too rude, I accepted them and quietly gave them to a friend who owned a cleaning business and came and cleaned for me once a month. She was Catholic, and I was sure she would love them.

Little did I know that angels were conspiring to get me to read the Volumes. Of course they found their way back into my home. Mary and I had worked on the silent auction for the home for unwed mothers we had visited. I had mentioned several times that I intended to bid on this beautiful mahogany wooden carving which had been hand-made and donated to the fundraiser. I specifically expressed my desire to outbid everyone else, no matter what the cost. Mary made a beautiful basket to go with the wooden carving, and inside the basket was another set of the Volumes.

But by this time, Mary had called in the big guns. She asked a very dear old friend if she would intervene and personally ask me to read them. I had known this friend for years. This friend knew me when I was still rough and tumble and smoking and swearing. She had always treated me like I was a class act. She and I had worked together for years, and I missed her friendship terribly as she had been in Ireland for the past several years. So when Mary recruited her to call me directly and tell me it was important that I reconsider reading the books, I did. "Well, of course

I will if you think I should," I said. "I am a reasonable person and it is just that I am not Catholic. But if you think I should read them, then I will."

So I told her I would read them. Oh, my goodness, now I had promised her that I would read these books so I better find the time. Do they not realize I have a grandchild on the way? Do they not realize how busy I am? Okay. A promise is a promise. These two women were really good friends to me and there must be a good reason why they are making this request, I thought.

I picked up Volume One and started to read it. Easy read, I thought. As I read on I got to a page where I swear I read these words (or at least they seemed to appear on the page), "*Abortion makes Jesus very sad, and then it makes Him angry, why would you want to do anything that would make Jesus sad and angry.*"

Tears flowed from my eyes as I continued to read Volume One. This was too much for me to bear. It hit me hard. God cared about me so much that long ago He placed this Irish Catholic girlfriend in my life. He has continued to care about me to the extent that He would have these girls track me down and make me see how much He loves me and how clearly my earthly actions and activities could/ would/did hurt Him, actually break His heart in two.

I vowed right then and there that I would never do anything ever again to promote or facilitate the abortion movement, and I would start to spread the word, the true word that these are children that belong to God. No one on earth has the right to prevent their birth, let alone deliberately kill them, ripping them out of their mother's womb. You may think that sounds harsh. But let's be real, shall we? An abortion is the killing of a baby, plain and simple. You cannot put enough lipstick on that pig to change that fact.

"Okay, Lord, I finally get it. What a wild ride. But just so we're clear, I am not converting to Catholicism. I am fine in my own little Lutheran world." That is the message I sent up to God, loud and precise. I am sure Jesus smiled.

A MASS IN A HOUSE?

Mary had more work assigned to her, and she did not even know it. Being the good Irish Catholic girl that she was, she kept me close so God could work through her. Our good friend from Ireland was coming to the States for a visit, and Mary and one of her priest friends decided to have a Mass at her house while our friend was in town. I was invited. Strange, I thought to have a Mass at someone's house. Was this even possible? And I was invited. Really weird, I thought. We Lutherans go to church. Period. A Mass at someone's house? Well I would go out of respect and since I was not Catholic, what could possibly happen anyway?

As I entered Mary's home, all five of her kids were there helping her to get everything ready for the Mass. I said hello to everyone and sat down in the back of the room. Mary had set up folding chairs in her living room for the Mass. I sat down in the back as I was not Catholic and I though it respectful to let them all sit in the front.

The Mass began. Not too different from the Lutheran Church, as far as I could see. After all, Martin Luther had been Catholic himself, so he probably brought a lot of it with him, right? Besides, even I knew that all Christians worshiped the same Jesus and that Jesus loved us all the same. I had been in different Christian Churches in my lifetime, and we all love Jesus. Even Catholics loved Jesus, so I was cool with it.

When the time came for Holy Communion, I sat in my chair while everyone else went up. Even I knew that if you were not Catholic you would not take Holy Communion at a Catholic Mass. As I sat there, warmth welled up inside me and tears came to my eyes as I felt Jesus apologizing to me saying, "I am so sorry that you cannot come to my table." It was like I was breaking His heart all over again, and I knew it was because I had not availed myself of the Holy Eucharist through the Catholic Church. The tears rolled down my face, past my sunglasses that I had put on to try to hide them.

I could not even wait for the Mass to be over so I could find Mary and tell her of my experience and announce that I now knew that I wanted to convert to the Catholic Church. When Mass was ended, I made my way over to her to deliver my big news. Upon hearing my proclamation, she said, "That's great" as she walked into her kitchen. What? That's it? I give her this big announcement and she walks away? Okay, I guess since she was hosting a Mass and other people were there, she needed to talk to them and look after her kids.

I pursued her into the kitchen and again stressed this miracle that had just occurred within me and sought her advice on how to covert to the Catholic Church. Surely this was pleasing to her. Surely she would want to help me in every way she could. To my utter surprise she suggested I find a Catholic Church and start taking RCIA classes. WHAT? Are you kidding me? You hound me like a dog regarding abortion so I can see the error of my ways? You and God move heaven and earth to get me to read the Volumes? You invite me to a Catholic Mass at you house and now when I have this epiphany, I am on my own?

Find a Church?

Take RCIA classes?

"Fine, missy, I can do that," I said as I walked away fuming.

The nerve of that girl, I thought.

I did not understand at that moment that I needed to find my own way and that it would make the adventure so much more pleasing to God and to me if I became a grownup where my faith was concerned.

I had always thought I had faith like a child, and I believe that God enjoys those of us who do, but now it was time for me to grow up in my faith all the while keeping the love I had for Jesus as a little child.

RCIA—JOINING THE CATHOLIC CHURCH

On September 1 little Gabriel, my first grandchild was born. His name was given to him by his father, and I believe it came right from heaven. I was in the process of finding a Catholic Church so I could begin these RCIA classes, as I had been instructed by Mary. I remembered seeing a lady from the courthouse at a retirement party for a local priest who was an activist from St. Anne's Catholic Church. I had represented him in court after he had gotten himself arrested for trespassing in an act of civil disobedience. Ms. Ethel had been at the party, and now she was at the courthouse. What a coincidence. I asked her how I would become Catholic, and she immediately picked up the phone and called her good friend Vesta who just happened to be the RCIA Director at St. Anne's Catholic Church. I could not make this stuff up.

Ms. Ethel arranged for me to meet her at church on that Sunday as the classes would start in October and she thought it a good idea for me to meet Vesta prior to the classes. Okay, so maybe I was not really on my own after all. Anyway, the only instruction Ms. Ethel gave me for Sunday was to meet her in the vestibule in the front of the church at 8:30 am. I could do that. Simple enough, right?

Sunday morning arrived and I was at St. Anne's in the vestibule at 8:15 a.m. sharp. Mass was to begin at 8:30 a.m., and I did not like to be late. Little did I know that being late did not bother Ms. Ethel. I stood in the vestibule and waited and waited for what seemed like an eternity. All of a sudden I heard a voice in my head. This was not the kind and loving voice I had heard in my heart on previous occasions. Jesus talks to us in our hearts, the evil one tends to work on our heads. No, this one was an evil, scary voice telling me that I did not belong there and that Ms. Ethel had forgotten about me and I would be embarrassed and humiliated because I did not even know when to kneel or when to stand and everyone would know that I was not Catholic.

At that very moment, I burst into tears. A kind gentleman who was serving as an usher stopped and asked me if I was all right. "No, of course I am not all right," I said, "I am waiting for Ms. Ethel and she is not here and I am not Catholic and…" He saw my tears and did what any smart man would do. He ran into the church and got his wife.

She was so kind and took me by the arm and had me sit with her. She helped me to follow along during the service and made me feel very welcome. I did not know much, but I was smart enough to figure out that Satan did not want me there and had tried everything he could to try to stop me from entering the church.

Luckily, God had my back, and so did the usher, Clarence. Remember Clarence the angel from *It's A Wonderful Life* with Jimmy Stewart? And so it went. I started my classes in October, and in November the devil tried plan #2 to stop my conversion.

IT AIN'T JUST
THE FLU THIS TIME

The week before Thanksgiving I started feeling weak but just chalked it up to a cold. Then on the Monday before Thanksgiving I knew I was really sick. I had failed to get a flu shot that year, and since I had not eaten all weekend I had gotten to the point where I passed out a few times the day before. Oh, it must be that dastardly flu, I thought, but this was really starting to get the best of me. My mom came over, took one look at me, and insisted I call my doctor. I spoke to my doctor who instructed us to come right into her office immediately. When we arrived, she too knew something was very wrong. My blood pressure was abnormally low, and my doctor sent us to the emergency room at the hospital across the street from her office as she called ahead to alert them to my condition.

AN ILLUSTRATION OF GRACE

My husband Joe was working midnights at the police station in our town which was over forty miles away. Because we are still thinking that this is just a severe case of the flu, my mom drove home and I was admitted into St. James hospital, you guessed it, a Catholic hospital with Channel 4 the Mass channel running in my room 24/7, although at times I was too weak to even appreciate it.

It was around midnight after a CAT scan and another ultrasound of my heart that it was discovered that I had a large amount of fluid surrounding my heart, crushing it, to be exact. It was pericarditis which had developed into cardiac tamponade, and the young residents, with tears in their eyes, came into my room to tell me that I should really get my husband down to the hospital as fast as possible because I may not make it until the morning.

WHAT?

Oh, come on, I just got a grandchild, and I was on the road to converting to Catholicism. Well at least I was in a Catholic hospital, I thought.

Within hours I was rushed into a room where my doctor and the chief cardiologist were waiting. They calmly explained that they would have to drain the fluid off my heart, and fast, or my heart would literally be crushed under the weight of the fluid. Now I knew I had gained a few pounds lately but I thought it might have more to do with the Twinkies as I was unaware of this massive amount of fluid present.

"Okay," I said, "so drain the fluid." I was thinking to myself, how hard could that be?

The doctors proceeded to explain to me that the only way they could drain the fluid was to stick a large needle directly into my chest and drain it into a pitcher.

What? You have got to be kidding me. That was going to hurt like hell. This was like a scene out of M*A*S*H!

In went the needle. Out came the liquid. My screams could be heard throughout the hospital. They inserted a tube into my chest for the rest of the fluid to drain off during the night, and I was administered morphine. I was in so much pain I thought I was going to die. But, no, I was not going to die as they had managed to relive the pressure off my heart just in time.

I spent the rest of the week hooked up to tubes and drugs until I was strong enough to go home.

I had only missed two of my RCIA classes and since I was the only student in the class, Vesta was kind enough to arrange make-up sessions.

I was on my way.

EASTER FINALLY ARRIVES

Time past quickly and soon it was Easter, a blessed time, a joyous time, and, for me this year, my confirmation on Holy Saturday at the Easter Vigil Service. I arrived at church in the morning to rehearse the ceremony since I had never seen one before. I wanted to make sure I knew exactly what was going to take place. As Vesta and I went though the motions of the rehearsal, Father Kevin came into the church all exicted. He was giddy, like a little kid.

"Guess what?" he said, "Guess who is getting confirmed with you tonight?"

"No one, Father," I told him confidently, "I was in the class all by myself."

"It's Clarence," he said, "Clarence is getting confirmed tonight as well."

Clarence was the usher, the man who had helped me that first day in the vestibule, Clarence, my angel.

As it turned out, Clarence had gone through RCIA many years ago but was never confirmed. Oh my goodness, God is certainly smiling today, I thought. God's plans for us are so good and way too involved for me to ever understand, but one thing I do know is that His love for us never fails.

My entire family came to my confirmation along with some dear friends and, of course, Mary.

ONE BIG CHRISTIAN FAMILY

My grandson Gabriel was baptized in the Catholic Church by Father Kevin and is now attending Catholic grade school.

Joey is in college in a nearby state, and we see him quite often.

My husband is retired from the police department and works at a Catholic high school as a school safety officer.

My oldest daughter is engaged to a man from Ghana whose cousin is a Catholic priest. I now have two more grandsons in Virginia, Zion and Messayah.

My mom and younger daughter completed RCIA with Vesta. I was my mom's sponsor, and Joey was Samantha's sponsor. They were confirmed this past Easter on Holy Saturday with the entire family in church, five years after my confirmation.

As I worked on this book, I wondered, what's next Lord?

Just then, Jesus reminded me, as He always does as He answers my questions as quickly as my thoughts, deep in my heart I hear Him, *"Finish the book and I will tell you."*